# IRISH AMERICANS

## ETHNIC GROUPS IN AMERICAN LIFE SERIES

Milton M. Gordon, *editor*

| | |
|---|---|
| *ANDERSON* | WHITE PROTESTANT AMERICANS: From National Origins to Religious Group |
| *FALLOWS* | IRISH AMERICANS: Identity and Assimilation |
| *FITZPATRICK* | PUERTO RICAN AMERICANS: The Meaning of Migration to the Mainland |
| *KITANO* | JAPANESE AMERICANS: The Evolution of a Subculture, Second Edition |
| *LOPATA* | POLISH AMERICANS: Status Competition in an Ethnic Community |
| *MOORE* | MEXICAN AMERICANS: Second Edition |
| *PINKNEY* | BLACK AMERICANS: Second Edition |
| *WAX* | INDIAN AMERICANS: Unity and Diversity |

# IRISH

*MARJORIE R. FALLOWS*
Cape Cod Community College

# AMERICANS

*Identity*

*and*

*Assimilation*

PRENTICE-HALL, INC., ENGLEWOOD CLIFFS, N.J. 07632

*Library of Congress Cataloging in Publication Data*

Fallows, Marjorie R. (date).
Irish Americans.

(Prentice-Hall ethnic groups in American life series)
Includes bibliographical references and index.
1. Irish Americans—Social conditions.
2. Irish Americans—Ethnic identity. I. Title.
E184.I6F24 301.45'19'162073 78-23323
ISBN 0-13-506261-6
ISBN 0-13-506253-5 pbk.



*Printed in the United States of America*

*10 9 8 7 6 5 4 3 2 1*

PRENTICE-HALL INTERNATIONAL, INC., *London*
PRENTICE-HALL OF AUSTRALIA PTY. LIMITED, *Sydney*
PRENTICE-HALL OF CANADA, LTD., *Toronto*
PRENTICE-HALL OF INDIA PRIVATE LIMITED, *New Delhi*
PRENTICE-HALL OF JAPAN, INC., *Tokyo*
PRENTICE-HALL OF SOUTHEAST ASIA PTE. LTD., *Singapore*
WHITEHALL BOOKS LIMITED, *Wellington, New Zealand*

*For my family:*
*Alden, Becky, Pam, and Denny,*
*whose understanding and good cheer*
*make anything possible.*

# Contents

# *Preface*

Irish Americans provide us with a case study of a predominantly Catholic ethnic group which has arrived at the threshold of full assimilation into American life. The struggle to reach this threshold contains many of the elements of a sociological adventure story, for it is rooted in a past that includes colonial exploitation, revolt, and famine, the splitting apart of families as migration to America became institutionalized, the transformation of rural peasants into industrial workers gathered for support and sociability in the first of America's urban ghettos, and the subsequent creation of influential religious, political, and social structures that have since been incorporated into American life. Far from having ceased to be of sociological interest, the experiences of these urban pioneers and their descendents provide us with an opportunity to analyze the stages involved in the complex assimilation process, to identify both the conditions necessary for transition from one stage to another and the social forces influencing the rate at which the transition might occur, and finally to assess the choices ahead for an ethnic group whose members are free to define their own identity.

Because the focus of this book is on the lives of ordinary people as they have been affected by social forces, this analysis of Irish Americans as an ethnic group combines three perspectives. The social analysis of history provides insight into the multiple reasons for the emigration from Ireland, the continued concern for Irish affairs on the part of those who had chosen life in America, and the continuities and contrasts between the Irish and American cultures in areas such as family life, politics, and religion. Sociological studies provide necessary data for delineating the shape and diversity of the Irish American subsociety, the avenues used for social mobility, and the problems encountered in the gradual journey toward full assimilation. And finally, firsthand accounts provided by oral histories and interviews trace the subjective definitions of situations that Irish Americans have faced, and provide a kind of composite family history of an ethnic group.

In combination, these approaches illuminate an ethnic journey that has been largely ignored by sociologists, and with which many Americans—even those of Irish ancestry—are little acquainted. It is a journey worth retracing, not because the Irish have provided the only or the best model for establishing an American identity in a pluralistic society, but because they have pioneered a route along which other ethnic Americans are still laboring in their various ways. For all of us there is, perhaps, a special insight to be gained from pausing and considering how one ethnic group which was initially considered different enough from the host society to be spurned as "outsiders" has gradually merged into the American social structure to the point where in most respects they regard themselves, and are regarded, as "insiders."

I am glad to be able to acknowledge here a longstanding intellectual debt to Milton M. Gordon, whose ideas have stimulated my concern for the ethnic experience, and whose editorial guidance has helped to shape that concern. I am grateful, too, for the assistance provided both by William V. D'Antonio, Project Director of the University of Connecticut's Ethnic Heritage Project: The Peoples of Connecticut, who encouraged my use of the Project's archives, and by Bruce M. Stave, Director of the Peoples of Connecticut Oral History Project, whose taped interviews with Irish Americans were especially helpful to me. Others whose advice and comments at various stages of manuscript preparation have proved valuable include Estelle Feinstein, John D. Murray, Thomas E. O'Connell, John Mulcahy, and Margaret and Burton Frost. Finally, there is no way to express adequately my appreciation to those members of the Irish-American community who shared their family histories and their thoughts with me. Although they remain anonymous on the written page, their contributions were unique and valued.

# IRISH AMERICANS

# CHAPTER ONE

# *Introducing the Irish Americans*

It has now been well over a century since towns and cities along the eastern seaboard of America reeled with the impact of the first massive wave of Irish Catholic immigrants fleeing famine conditions in their homeland. Nothing in past experience had prepared either native Americans or incoming Irish for the unexpected clash of social and religious styles that soon emerged in those communities where sizable numbers of the Irish settled. No students of ethnicity stood by to document the gradual steps by which the Irish came to be viewed, and to view themselves, as Americans. Moreover, by the time ethnicity became an area for serious sociological concern, the Irish simply no longer stood out as an ethnic group suffering the severe disadvantages of more recently discovered minorities. Their experience as the first conspicuously different ethnic wave in America came to be viewed as past history. What, after all, need one know about people whose assimilation has progressed to the point where they have very nearly become a lost statistical category?

A young Irish American friend protested this state of affairs to me a decade ago when he said, "My name is Kelly, but beyond knowing the Irish songs that every American kid learns I hardly know what it means to be Irish. Here are the blacks with their history and their problems, and the Puerto Ricans with theirs, but what happened to mine?" This study will attempt to answer my young friend's question, for today we recognize that ethnicity is a resilient form of social life, capable of surprising metamorphoses. We may even have been hasty in proclaiming the demise of the Irish Americans as a self-conscious ethnic group.

The largely Catholic Irish of the famine years were not, of course, the first Irish to have immigrated to America. They had been preceded during the seventeenth and eighteenth centuries by smaller numbers of their countrymen, many of whom had been Protestants from the northern county of Ulster who had come under less dramatic circumstances and who had been socially, religiously, and culturally quite similar to the existing American population. In fact, many of those in this earlier "Ulster migration" had arrived in time to help Americans win their independence from England, against which they too had deep resentments, and by the mid-1800s the majority regarded themselves, and were regarded, as members of the Anglo-

American host society. This is not to deny their Irish origin: They had established Irish organizations in the major cities of America by the mid-1800s, and their present-day descendants may, when asked, still note that they are of Irish extraction—though perhaps more as a point of historical interest than as an identification with social relevance for their lives. Nonetheless, this earliest group of Irish immigrants are not our primary concern. They will figure in our discussion as a minor theme and only at those points where their Irishness emerges as significant for them and for the later-arriving Irish Catholics with whom they can be compared.

These later-arriving "famine immigrants" were, of course, not the last to emigrate from Ireland to America, for by the time the worst of the famine years were over the journey to America had become institutionalized as a way of life. Nearly every family in Ireland has sent one or more of its members to America in what has become one of the longest lasting and most remarkable examples of serial migration in America's history. These later immigrants—the majority of them young single men and women—came not only for the adventure and for better opportunities, but also because they had relatives already here who spoke a common language and who encouraged them to come.

The popular wisdom which regards nearly all Irish Americans as descended from the Catholic peasants who came at the time of the potato famine may be factually incorrect, but in terms of the emotional bonds that created a sense of Irish American peoplehood it is close to the truth. The distinctive characteristics that made the Irish American community unique, and that determined the kind of experience the Irish and their descendants would have in America, were the characteristics of those who emigrated after 1830. The drama and change experienced by these Catholic Irish as they transformed themselves from rural peasants to urban workers provide clues to understanding both the complex assimilation process and the enduring need for ethnic identity. This study, then, is a sociological exploration of the present status of these Irish Americans, viewed from the perspective of the long and bitter history which helped to shape it.

Let us begin where hundreds of Irish immigrants did—in the mid-1800s, in one of the many Atlantic seaboard communities whose future was to be deeply affected by the incoming Irish. In the heart of Bridgeport, Connecticut, there is a small abandoned Irish Catholic cemetery, the Cemetery of St. James.[1] The name on a weathered tombstone shows that, in midwinter of 1836, Rose Ann Masterson was the first to be buried in this consecrated plot of land on what was then Cook's Lane. Three years later the grave was dug for John Neville of Macroom, County Cork, to be followed in the next five decades by others from the Irish Catholic community

[1] Full information on the Cemetery of Saint James is contained in the 1938 *WPA Federal Writers' Project on the Growth of Bridgeport, Connecticut* (Storrs: Ethnic Heritage Project: The Peoples of Connecticut, 1975).

who would never return to County Tipperary, Westmeath, or Galway again. Patrick Callahan and Mary Hagerty died in their twenties, before whatever hopes they brought with them from Ireland could be fulfilled. Patrick Hogan and John Burke fought in the Irish Regiment of the Connecticut Volunteers during the Civil War. Michael Cleary and his wife Mary died in their eighties, an ocean away from relatives in County Limerick.

We will never know what brought them all from their homes in Ireland, for St. James Church has disappeared from church records and just the cemetery remains to tell of those who formed this early Irish community. The tombstones show only that they began their lives in Ireland, as early as the time of the American Revolution, and ended them in this small American city. Their children, if any, might have been buried in the cemetery of the more imposing St. Augustine's Church of Bridgeport, which succeeded St. James, or more likely in the Catholic cemeteries of other American cities across the country where Irish men followed the work on roads, canals, and railroads, while young Irish women started as domestics in the homes of Anglo Americans and later raised families in the first immigrant ghettos American cities had seen. The unlucky ones died of exhaustion or fever on construction gangs, the lucky ones made fortunes in gold or silver, and the enterprising developed skills in business and politics. If some of the descendants of such as Michael and Mary Cleary live comfortably in the suburbs of Hartford, St. Paul, and San Francisco, concerned about which college their children should attend, considering a pilgrimage to find their roots in County Limerick, and attending Mass in their parish churches with vague misgivings about all the changes introduced by Vatican II, others doubtless still remain in the old Irish neighborhoods that have been abandoned by their more prosperous friends.

The Cemetery of St. James speaks both of an end and a beginning for the Irish in America. The adventurous had escaped a rural past of disappointment, had chosen the urban centers of an expanding American economy, had formed their neighborhoods around memories and hopes they shared with fellow Irish countrymen and women, and had persevered in the hope that their children and grandchildren would prosper. Although millions of immigrants from scores of other countries have followed, the Irish comprised the first wave of those who were different in their religion, in their rejection of the rural life, and in the antagonism they aroused in, and felt toward, the dominant Anglo-Americans, so similar in their outlook to the hated British conquerors. As the first, they set a pattern which, in many ways, has become familiar to other later groups.

Some would contend that the Irish have merged into the American mainstream, leaving only such reminders of their passing as the abandoned Cemetery of St. James, the parades on St. Patrick's day, or, more importantly, the structure of urban political machines and the character of the

Catholic Church in America. Others would point out that in this passage they have become a different breed, distinct from the Irish who remained in Ireland, whom they now outnumber. After all, it was they who found the courage to leave rather than stay; it was they who survived the struggle to carve out a place for those of Catholic faith in a Protestant country; it was they who won the economic and political power needed to assure their countrymen here of a decent place in America and their countrymen in Ireland of support in their struggle for independence from England. They were doers.

In the process of all this, most descendants of the Irish immigrants have come to feel at ease and accepted as Americans, having symbolically "arrived" when they provided their adopted country with one of their own as President. If any immigrant group can be said to have merged into the American social structure to the point where neither they nor the host society any longer cares to dwell on presumed ethnic differences or to limit participation in any area of life because of them, this may well be true of the Irish American descendants of such as Michael and Mary Cleary. The purpose of this book is to investigate whether this really has happened and, if so, to trace how.

## THE FIRST "DIFFERENT" IMMIGRANT WAVE

In the memories of many American families, the immigrant passage from the old to the new country takes on some of the same mythical significance as the legend of the Flood, which reminds people in farflung places that their ancestors experienced a cataclysmic event that changed the world they knew. Those who survive such cataclysms take on heroic proportions as the years pass. A young Irish American woman, discussing her immigrant ancestors, expressed this sense of awe when she said:

> When I think of these mere children, younger than I am, who left home for good at twelve or sixteen and who worked as maids and kept boarding houses, and hauled cement and dug canals, and raised families, and made good here—it seems as though they must have been very special.[2]

However little is known of those in the immigrant generation—and many Americans know remarkably little—there is a common awareness that our lives are totally changed because of them.

As immigrants, the Irish had the misfortune to be the first in a tide of those who would be categorized as different enough from the Anglo-American mold to raise serious questions about their adaptability.

[2] Marjorie R. Fallows, private interview with a third-generation Irish American, 1975.

Pressures of overpopulation, domination by a foreign power, political and religious persecution, economic dislocation, crop failure—all these were components in the exodus of the Irish from their native land, as they have been for countless others arriving in America. But alongside these pressures to leave the old country were strong enticements to migrate to the new: passage money from relatives who had already made the journey, glorified accounts of the opportunities that awaited the adventurous in the new country. With few prospects at home, and little hope for improved conditions, the flow of Irish immigration began even before the American Revolution, rose to a flood between 1835 and 1855, and became institutionalized as a way of Irish and American life in the years that followed. By the time immigration quotas were established in the 1920s, the Irish were already regarded as among the early settlers whose Americanization was no longer in serious doubt.

A massive transplant of peoples had occurred—a splitting of families into their Irish and American contingents who would continue side by side on opposite shores of the Atlantic, affecting each other's destinies but committed to different ways of life. To describe the Irish as immigrants, then, is to recognize that they were also emigrants from a land whose future was dramatically affected by their departure. The immigrant's tale is always the tale of two countries.

## A SENSE OF PEOPLEHOOD

To describe the Irish as an ethnic group in America requires a little more explanation, for the concept of ethnicity has acquired a variety of usages. Most simply, an ethnic group is comprised of people who are socially differentiated on the basis of race, religion, or national origin, who develop a subsociety within which most significant social interaction can occur, and who share a sense of their own peoplehood.[3] Ethnicity is an intergroup concept, for an ethnic group is so defined because it is recognized as socially different from some other existing group.

For the Irish, the long experience of domination by the English in their homeland had created a sense of peoplehood which may well have accentuated ethnic identity beyond that felt by less persecuted peoples. Although numerically in the majority, they were a subjugated people who were constantly reminded that they were considered culturally inferior, racially degenerate, and religiously misled. Those Irish who emigrated were already well aware of the hazards of being in the wrong ethnic category. As immigrants, they soon discovered that such patterns of discrimination were not unique to the old country.

[3] For an elaboration of the concept of "ethnic group" see Milton Gordon, *Assimilation in American Life* (New York: Oxford University Press, 1964), pp. 23–30.

By contemporary definitions of race, the Irish would not have been regarded as racially distinct from the Anglo-Americans among whom they found themselves, but contemporary definitions did not apply in the eighteenth and nineteenth centuries. Culturally acquired characteristics were assumed to be transmitted in the blood, and the Irish were cavalierly described as a race which preferred to live in the filth of hovels, which was innately contentious and brawling and criminal, and which showed few signs of being able to respond to civilizing influences. Thus, although they were physically similar to the Anglo-Saxons, many Irish had been so systematically deprived of education and training for any but the simplest rural pursuits that their lack of skills reinforced the image of racial inferiority.

Religiously, they were the first large ethnic wave to America which brought Catholicism as an integral part of its culture. Having resisted the pressures to convert to Protestantism at home, they had no intention of abandoning their faith, in spite of American anti-Catholic feeling which had its source in the British origins of the Anglo Americans with whom they interacted. Although American colonists had had political differences with Britain, they had retained many of the anti-Catholic, and particularly anti-Irish Catholic, attitudes that had prevailed in England at the time of their departure. Thus, the Irish Catholics in America found their Anglo-Saxon hosts virtually as intolerent of their Catholicism as the English had been.

Those Protestant Irish who had emigrated earlier for economic reasons were quick to sense the advantage in disassociating themselves from their Catholic compatriots. The term Scotch-Irish came to identify the Protestant Irish as a separate, and largely acceptable, ethnic group which merged more quickly into American life. It was not the national origin component of ethnicity, then, that automatically relegated the Irish to an inferior position, but the Catholic religious component which came to represent the critical factor making them seem strange, suspect, and therefore to be set apart. From a majority ethnic group fighting for survival in Ireland, the Irish immigrants to America became a minority ethnic group struggling not only for survival but also for respectability in an overwhelmingly Anglo-Saxon Protestant country. The sense of peoplehood was already there; the creation of a subculture evolved as part of the means of survival.

## ANGLO EXPECTATIONS FOR IMMIGRANTS

Since a subculture involves a way of life in which much, if not all, subsocietal interaction takes place, it might, in its most persistent form, prevent the immigrant's having any significant interaction with the host society at all. Yet such extreme isolation seldom occurs, and certainly it did not for the Irish at any stage of their long experience in this country. Although a minority of immigrants who came from the isolated western counties of Ireland initially spoke only Irish (Gaelic), the majority were already familiar with the English language and ways, and all were practiced in survival tactics. The Irish quickly adapted to the outward forms of American culture, retaining only their Catholicism as a conspicuously different cultural feature. If all that were required for assimilation into American life were superficial acculturation, as has sometimes been assumed, the story would be complete. Yet it was far from that, as the Irish were to discover.

Part of the subtler acculturation process involves the absorption of the host group's current ideologies to explain the way things are. The ideologies, as they applied to immigrants, took several distinct forms to which the Irish of each period had to respond. At first, it was assumed that all immigrants would naturally conform to the dominant Anglo American norms, and it was into this climate of thinking that the first great wave of Irish immigrants disembarked in the first half of the nineteenth century. Groups clearly unable to adapt because of racial differences or cultural preferences would, it became apparent, be as much beyond the pale as those Irish who were forever squatters on their own land beyond the English-controlled garrison strip called the Pale in Ireland. To have been fully acceptable in the Pale, an Irishman must have renounced his Catholicism and his compatriots—in short, denied his peoplehood. Few would submit, even in exchange for the rewards in education, wealth, and power that were offered. Anglo conformity was clearly an ideology well understood but little appreciated by the Irish in America, and most damaging for those who remained in centers like Boston, where it long dominated the thinking of a tight Anglo American community,

Although the Irish Catholics were less prone to venture to the wilderness frontiers than the earlier Irish Protestants (Scotch-Irish), it was those frontiers which provided the conditions for a second ideology encountered by immigrants. According to the somewhat romanticized melting pot thesis, all Americans would merge to make a new hybrid type, taking the best of all that was offered from immigrants and earlier settlers alike and emerging as a dynamic breed fired in the forge of the frontier. Like all myths, that of the melting pot contained an element of truth as well as an element of desire, but the Irish unequivocally avoided the frontier. Preferring to settle in urban centers along the Atlantic coast where their lack of skills left them less vulnerable to total disaster, they found themselves socially segregated—by choice and by necessity—and little affected by any melting pot process that might be occurring elsewhere. Indeed, only by grouping together and serving their own needs did they see the possibility of succeeding.

Both of these major ideologies that have been proposed to explain the assimilation of ethnic minorities were unrealistic for the majority of the Irish. Anglo conformity paralleled too closely the capitulation to English dominance in their homeland, especially as it involved the expectation that they would abandon their Catholicism, and the melting pot did not describe the segregated ethnic enclaves that had formed in American cities where the Irish primarily settled. Indeed, as later waves of immigrants followed in Irish footsteps it became apparent that assimilation could be a complex and agonizing affair both for the newcomers and for the receiving society. Bravely begun, it might still falter or be rejected at almost any stage along the way.

## THE STAGES OF ASSIMILATION

By the mid-twentieth century, social scientists began taking official note of a persistent ethnic pluralism in American society. Although sometimes referred to as cultural pluralism, this phenomenon could seldom be attributed to a failure in acculturation. Like the Irish, nearly all but the most recent immigrants had made enthusiastic progress toward behavioral assimilation, yet they were not fully included in the institutional life and intimate social affairs of the Anglo-American host society. Parallel but separate social structures had evolved to serve the needs of ethnic subsocieties, created first by necessity and perpetuated later by habit or choice.

Because such pluralism was not what the ideologies had prepared us to expect, it was not until Milton Gordon's careful analysis of the assimilation process in *Assimilation in American Life* that structural assimilation was identified as the most crucial, yet least recognized, stage in the experience of an ethnic group.[4] Without full incorporation into the social affairs of the host society, at a primary level, not only would merging through intermarriage be unlikely but consciousness of the differences between in-group and out-group would tend to perpetuate the prejudice and discrimination which seem inevitably to attach to diverse perceptions of peoplehood.

Indeed, it has become apparent that there have been twin strains marking the relationships between ethnic subsocieties and the host society in American experience. While some, such as tribal Indian groups or the Amish people, have forcefully resisted pressures to assimilate, others have moved willingly toward assimilation, only to find that institutionalized barriers prevented full participation in their adopted society. Nor are these twin strains of accommodation—forced assimilation with resistance from the subordinate group, and attempted assimilation with resistance from the dominant group—solely an American phenomenon. As Richard

[4] *Ibid.,* Ch. 3.

Schermerhorn has pointed out, conflict in intergroup situations is most likely to arise precisely when there is lack of agreement about the desirability of assimilation as a goal.[5] If both groups agree—either to remain separate and different, or to become as one—the occasion for conflict is reduced. Thus even structural pluralism, the maintenance of separate institutions and social lives, may be defined as normal and desirable in a multi-ethnic society if all groups involved feel their best interests are served. Emerging American ideology does not discount this possibility.

It is one of the ironies of the Irish experience in America that only when they had demonstrated superior success in conforming to Anglo-American norms did the Irish discover that ethnic pride was acceptable—even to be desired. Andrew Greeley has said:

> The legitimation of ethnicity came too late for the American Irish. They are the only European immigrant group to have over-acculturated. They stopped being Irish the day before it became all right to be Irish. The WASPS won the battle to convert the Irish into WASPS, just before the announcement came that permanent peace had been made with ethnic diversity.[6]

Whether Greeley has overstated the case remains perhaps to be seen. But few would contest the fact that the Irish in this country provide a case study of a group whose stages of adjustment are more nearly complete than most others'. Variations along regional, rural/urban, and social class lines exist, to be sure, and the time elapsed since the original immigrant generation provides further variations in the Irish community. But if there is a sequence in the stages through which an immigrant group passes on the way to acceptance, the Irish may serve to illustrate what it is and to identify the conditions for transition from one stage to another.

But before we begin to trace the Irish American experience in America, one caution is in order. It is the purpose of social analysis to search out identifiable patterns in human interaction and to account for the variations that inevitably occur, yet no Irish immigrants saw themselves as part of a pattern which could, for instance, be labeled "the famine generation." The pattern emerges only in perspective and is seldom perceived by those who live the experience. For participants it seems that events might easily have gone another way, had they themselves but chosen differently. But while choice is one side of the human condition, it is also true that people who choose apparently independent courses frequently find themselves on the same path, responding to pressures beyond their control and social structural conditions of which they are barely aware.

[5] Richard A. Schermerhorn, *Comparative Ethnic Relations* (New York: Random House, 1970).

[6] Andrew Greeley, *That Most Distressful Nation* (Chicago: Quadrangle Books, 1973), p. 263.

Where free choice and predestination cross is the area in which sociological inquiry operates.

As with every other immigrant group, the Irish who came to America were actors making their choices, fulfilling their perceived roles, moving into emergent ones as their personal capabilities interacted with the social structure around them, and coming to terms with their ethnic identity as part of themselves. The extent to which their ethnicity was something of which they were proud or ashamed, which helped or hindered them in their search for dignity and success, which was clung to because it mattered or jettisoned because it was no longer relevant, illuminates the long journey the Irish Americans have made.

CHAPTER TWO

# The Irish Inheritance

The people of Ireland live with an ancient past. How long ago Irishmen first made tentative contact with North America may never be known, but Irish legends of the pre-Christian era tell of enchanted islands far in the western ocean while Irish tradition tells of monks of the seventh and eighth centuries who pursued their missionary efforts in lands to the west.[1] Ancient tales of Celtic kings and warriors who lived two hundred years before Christ, of the splendid conversion of Ireland to Christianity by its patron, St. Patrick, and of the art and poetry that flourished in Irish monasteries and courts while Medieval Europe slept, all remind the people of Ireland that there have been more heroic days.

Max Caulfield, who wonders whether this link with an extraordinarily ancient past does not give a unique perspective on life, has written of the Irishman:

> He is not unique in possessing a body of ancient saga—but he is unique in that it has perhaps more meaning for him because of the intense efforts made to wipe out the culture that created it. The heroic image of a warrior caste has persisted, therefore—honed and sharpened by centuries of resistance to Britain.[2]

Having lived as an unwilling subject people nearly five times longer than the United States has even existed as a nation, the Irish still never accepted the inevitability of their subjugation. Caulfield observes that:

> No other nation in Europe has harbored such a long and sullen resentment against its conquerors. The Irish memory still rankles at defeat, wrestles to understand how and why it was unable to eject a foreigner, sighs over lost chances, and debates bitterly why certain victory always and inevitably turned to catastrophic defeat.[3]

The survival of the Irish sense of peoplehood through nearly one thousand years of conquest can perhaps best be understood by recognizing that an extraordinary cultural unity in language, law, and religion had developed throughout Ireland by the year 800 but that without a matching

[1] William D. Griffin, *The Irish in America: A Chronology and Fact Book* (Dobbs Ferry, N.Y.: Oceana Publications, Inc., 1972), p.1.

[2] Max Caulfield, *The Irish Mystique* (Englewood Cliffs, N.J.: Prentice-Hall, 1973), p. 91.

[3] *Ibid.,* p. 141.

political unity there was virtually no way to protect it from outside attack in the years that followed.[4] The competing and often antagonistic clans could be easily defeated by their own lack of unity and organization, yet because they were difficult, if not impossible, to govern, the Irish retained a highly developed sense of ethnic consciousness in the constant expectation that the conquerors would be driven off. The Vikings of the ninth and tenth centuries, who conquered and pillaged much of the island, had little lasting impact beyond such coastal trading towns as Dublin, Cork, Limerick, and Waterford. After eventually expelling the Vikings in 1014, however, the Irish were torn apart by internal feuds and then occupied some 150 years later by the Anglo-Normans, ushering in seven centuries of foreign domination. Although not all of Ireland was brought under effective English rule until 1603, when Hugh O'Neill surrendered to Mountjoy, the pattern of colonial domination dates back to the twelfth century.

The heroes of Irish history are those who led gallant, if futile, rebellions against the conquerors; those who developed verbal skills to procrastinate or to confuse the oppressors; those who later employed brilliant legal tactics to win political concessions. Seven hundred years is a stunning span of time to endure without giving in or giving up, but if the story of their subjugation is one of frustration and humiliation for the Irish, it is also one of confusion and anger for the British government. Those Englishmen sent to colonize and govern Ireland became, in fact, part of the British problem, although they were intended as part of the solution. By 1366, when it was feared that their obvious attraction to the Irish culture and people was jeopardizing their ability to remain separate and dominant, the members of the English colony were reminded of their duty by the Statutes of Kilkenny, which forbade them to marry the Irish, to use their language, their laws, their poets or minstrels, or any of the local customs. Already too late to halt the gradual identification of the English colonists with Irish interests, the British government found it had created for the future a separate Anglo-Irish faction which would add its discontent to that of the native Irish in later years.

With the coming of the Reformation in the sixteenth century, anti-Irish measures taken to enforce British domination and racial purity took on the added dimension of religious persecution. Henry VIII, the first English ruler to assume the title of King of Ireland, imposed the Acts of Supremacy on Ireland, and under subsequent monarchs the celebration of the Mass was made illegal and persecution of Catholics became wholesale. Widespread rebellion was punished by the British with such a slaughter of herds and destruction of crops that famine followed the revolt of 1579. Great sections of Munster, in the southwestern part of Ireland, were

[4] This section draws upon a number of historical sources including Edmund Curtis, *A History of Ireland* (New York: Barnes and Noble, Inc., 1960); and J.C. Beckett, *The Making of Modern Ireland, 1603–1923* (New York: Alfred A. Knopf, Inc., 1966).

"planted" with English Protestants, who were rewarded for their help in crushing the rebellion by being given Irish estates. Within twenty-five years a revolt in Ulster, in the northern part of Ireland, brought a similar "plantation" with Protestant Scotch and English settlers, following the defeat of the Irish nobles there and the "Flight of the Earls" to Europe in 1607. By the mid-1600s three-fourths of Irish lands had simply been transferred to Protestant loyalists, many of whom did not work their estates but remained in England as absentee landlords living off their Irish rents. The Irish masses had been stripped of the most basic human right and existed as serfs in their own land. The social structure of Ireland had been permanently altered.

In an attempt to secure once and for all the subjugation of the Catholic population, the Penal Laws, promulgated in 1695 and amended from time to time over the next century, denied Catholics the right to vote or hold office, barred them from teaching, trading, or entering the professions, and forbade them to bear arms. The remaining Catholic estates were further broken up through new restrictions on inheritance and ownership. With Catholic clergy and schools outlawed, the Catholic Church was driven underground. Mass was said in the fields, with lookouts posted to warn of approaching authorities; priests passed on their meager store of classical knowledge to children stealthily gathered about them in outdoor "hedge schools." Catholicism became an offense punishable by social, economic, and political deprivations intended to break the spirit and the strength of the Irish. Although the primary aim of the Penal Laws was to humiliate and demoralize the Irish Catholics as a people, rather than specifically to destroy Irish Catholicism, the strict enforcement of the political, social, and economic aspects of the Penal Laws was widely interpreted by Irish Catholics as an attempt to wipe out Catholicism in Ireland.

So complete was the economic stranglehold of the English on the Irish economy, in fact, that even Scotch and English Protestants in northern Ireland felt the squeeze and began to emigrate from Ulster to America, just in time to join the revolt of the American colonists against Britain. Meanwhile, the Anglo-Irish aristocracy in Dublin, to the south, had created an elegant and sophisticated urban culture in the Pale—that narrow strip of coastal Ireland dominated by Irish Protestants of English descent who were prospering at the expense of impoverished native Catholics.

More in response to the outrage of concerned Englishmen than because of any change in policy, the worst abuses of the Penal Lawswere gradually removed between 1778 and 1829, but their effects had been disastrous. The overwhelming majority of Irish Catholics were destitute, torn by seething resentments, and well versed in the survival techniques of the oppressed. They were able to maintain a sense of dignity only by perfecting their skills as masters of deception and dodgers of the law whose verbal skills confused and exasperated their overlords while amusing the knowing

Irish. This was the condition of Ireland when ships brought the astounding news that another oppressed colony of England's had finally accomplished what Ireland had only dreamed of. The American Revolution had succeeded! Somewhere in the western ocean that enchanted island of the legends really seemed to exist, or so it must have seemed to the million and more Irishmen who turned hopeful faces westward as they left their homeland for New York and Boston during the next century of mounting disaster in Ireland.

## THE GREAT FAMINE

To Irish on both sides of the Atlantic, the decades preceding and culminating in the Great Famine of 1845 to 1848 represent a watershed in their history. Popular tradition among the Irish regards the famine as man-made, for as Carl Wittke points out:

> the Irish believed that their lives had been sacrificed in the famine for the British merchant class, and that the British government, beholden to this class for their political support, was afraid to take effective steps to deal with the disaster, and, therefore, callously allowed Irishmen to die.[5]

Although there were Englishmen who were relieved to be able to consolidate Irish holdings by "shoveling out" tenants unable to pay the rents, and others who viewed the famine as fortuitous in bringing an end to the Irish population growth and reducing the numbers of restless natives, the English government did not invent the famine to serve its interests. Indeed, British "callousness" can best be understood by recognizing that England's famine policy was guided by the economic doctrine of laissez faire, which precluded governmental interference with commerce, and by analysis of the distinctive pattern of ethnic relations that had developed in Ireland under British colonial rule.

England had always viewed Ireland as a political threat, a possible springboard for European aggressors, and a center of intrigue for Catholic claimants to the English throne. As Robert Moore points out in his analysis of the roots of contemporary warfare in northern Ireland, "one of the main objects (if not *the* main object) of English policy was to secure Ireland politically and militarily."[6] Imposing Protestantism on unwilling Irishmen was initially seen as less important than making the Irish ruling class dependent on the Crown, but the constant fear that European Catholic powers would side with the Irish to drive out or destroy the British gradually focused concern on the religious factor.

[5] Carl Wittke, *The Irish in America* (New York: Russell and Russell, 1970), p. 8.
[6] Robert Moore, "Race Relations in the Six Counties: Colonialism, Industrialism, and Stratification in Ireland," in Norman Yetman and C. Hoy Steele (Eds.), *Majority and Minority* (Boston: Allyn and Bacon, Inc., 1975), p. 126.

Economically, the classic colonial situation prevailed, with less interest shown in developing Ireland than in exploiting it. Irish forests were cut down for timber and military use, the wool industry was gradually destroyed to prevent competition and provide a market for English wool, the land itself was exploited as a source of rent for absentee landlords and taxes for the Crown. As Moore makes clear, "Ireland was a British colony; dominated for England's political and economic advantage."[7]

With power vested in the English-dominated Protestant ruling class, and with the Irish Catholic nobility and middle classes fleeing to less austere conditions abroad, only the impoverished Catholic farmers remained of the native population in much of Ireland. In Ulster to the north, the Presbyterians originally brought from Scotland as part of the "plantation" effort had developed their own separate middle-class subculture, having little to do either with the Catholic natives or the Anglican English. Social stratification was augmented by religious cleavages: upper-class Anglicans, middle-class Presbyterians, and lower-class Catholics. Only after the vote was finally restored to the Catholics in 1793, and later mobilized behind Catholic emancipation candidates in the general election of 1826, did the two Protestant groups form an uneasy coalition in response to the fear of Catholic power. In the main, however, it was the ascriptive religious component that had become paramount in the distribution of wealth, prestige, and power. By any reckoning, the Catholic peasant farmers were relegated to a position of caste-like serfdom at the bottom.

There have been, and probably will continue to be, many instances of a numerically superior lower caste's being kept in paternalistic subjugation to a ruling elite. Pierre van den Berghe has enumerated the variables that might exist in an "ideal type" of the paternalistic colonial situation, and in it we find striking parallels with the Irish position just before the Great Famine.[8] We need only substitute the word *religious* for the word *racial* as the key variable in determining ascriptive status. The social structure would typically be agricultural, with division of labor following racial (religious) lines and allowing little mobility for the lower caste. The dominant aristocracy would be in the favored minority, yet there would be little ideological conflict about the rightness of the status quo, for this would be reinforced by the prevailing pattern of race (religious) relations, with its elaborate etiquette and sharply defined roles based on ascription. With the dominant group rationalizing its position by virtue of presumed racial and cultural superiority, often without distinguishing clearly between the two, and maintaining its power through a colonial form of government and separate legal status for the lower caste, the subordinate group would be stereotyped as inferior, childish, and irresponsible yet acceptable as long as

[7] *Ibid.*, p. 128

[8] Pierre L. van den Berghe, *Race and Racism: A Comparative Perspective* (New York: John Wiley and Sons, Inc., 1967), pp. 27–34.

the members stayed in their place. Van den Berghe points out that, with their elaborate ideology of racism and caste superiority, such regimes can show great resilience and longevity, for they are at least partially based on the acquiescence of the subordinate group.

Useful as the "ideal type" is in understanding the kind of colonial situation the British had attempted to create through the formation of a dominant Anglo-Irish Protestant ruling class in Ireland—which was in fact much harsher than English domination from abroad—it was clearly in the Irish refusal to accept the legitimacy of this domination that they deviated from the paternalistic model. The Irish, in short, indicated by their continued resistance to colonial rule that they intended to view their relations with England, and with its representatives in Ireland, as competitive rather than subservient, and in so doing they came to be viewed as insolent, aggressive, and underhanded in their challenging of the status quo. It may well be that other subject peoples have paid lip service to their conquerors' values with no more belief in them than the Irish displayed, but it was abundantly clear to the British that the Irish had not yet been, and perhaps never would be, spiritually broken.

The role of the family and of the Catholic Church in sustaining the Irish peasant's convictions during this period will be discussed in later chapters, but for now it is enough to say that Ireland, as it entered the years of the Great Famine, had reached a critical point in its history. Too close to England to be ignored, too rebellious to be tamed, the Irish plagued the British with politically unnerving and emotionally exhausting problems which seemingly would not go away. English patience with Irish problems was already thin when the potato blight struck.

The Great Famine was a phenomenon long in the making, not just a single catastrophic event.[9] Limited to farming by the British, the Irish had been forced to subdivide their meager family holdings and tenant plots of land into smaller and smaller parcels. With large families and no tradition of primogeniture, the land inherited by a son in the early 1800s might be as small as two or three acres. Potatoes were the only feasible crop, for on those few acres he could support a family of five or six, whereas corn or wheat would have required many times more land. Potatoes were well suited to the moist climate and simple space technology based on trench plantings with repeated earthing-up of the potato beds. In good years, the crop could not only support a family but provide food for pigs, chickens, and cattle, as well as providing a means of exchange in a society that as yet had no cash or money economy.

All years were not equally good, however, for the potato crop was as unstable as it was useful. Even in normal times, the summer months before

[9] For detailed and graphic accounts of the Great Famine see R. D. Edwards and T. D. Williams (Eds.), *The Great Famine: Studies in Irish History, 1845–52* (Dublin: Browne and Nolan, 1956); and Cecil Woodham-Smith, *The Great Hunger* (New York: Harper & Row, 1962).

harvest brought some degree of starvation for the improvident or the unlucky. Previous years of potato failures had accustomed the Irish to periodic famines in which thousands died. In fact, crop failures in various portions of the island had witnessed death, disease, subdivision of land, and emigration, which by the 1820s had already established patterns of movement and callous evictions. The Irish expected the overall 1845 harvest to be no better or worse than that of previous years. Instead, what appeared at first to be a bumper crop was struck early with a strange blight—freshly dug potatoes turned black and pulpy, disintegrating in an oily, foul-smelling ooze. At first reported in only a few districts, the blight was played down by the British government, but it gradually spread throughout nearly all of Ireland, totally destroying the staple food of the peasant and his domestic animals.

Chronicles of the time, written by both Irish and English who viewed the devastation, express the unbelieving shock of those surveying a battle scene. A traveler through the fertile center of Ireland on his way to Galway wrote of his journey:

> We saw sights that will never wholly leave the eyes that beheld them, cowering wretches almost naked in the savage weather, prowling in turnip fields, and endeavouring to grub up roots which had been left, but running to hide as the mailcoach rolled by: groups and families, sitting or wandering on the highroad, with failing steps, and dim, patient eyes, gazing hopelessly into infinite darkness and despair; parties of tall, brawny men, once the flower of Meath and Galway, stalking by with a fierce but vacant scowl; as if they realized that all this ought not to be, but knew not whom to blame, saw none whom they could rend in their wrath. Sometimes, I could see, in front of the cottages, little children leaning against a fence when the sun shone out—for they could not stand—their limbs fleshless, their bodies half-naked, their faces bloated yet wrinkled, and of a pale greenish hue—children who would never, it was too plain, grow up to be men and women.[10]

Starvation was followed by the inevitable diseases, and country lanes and urban centers alike were strewn with the bodies of Irish peasants and their farm animals. Amazingly, boatloads of grain from Irish farms continued to be shipped to England throughout the ten years of unrelieved famine. Unable to pay landlord or tax gatherer without the cash that the crops represented, those Irish who had fields of wheat or rye sold it to the British as they had done in the past. For some, it provided the only source of cash for the passage money to escape from Ireland itself.

At the end of the ten-year period of crop failure, Ireland's population stood at 6,500,000—two and one-half million short of what it would have been with normal growth. These were the Irish who had emigrated, died, or never been born. Ireland would never be the same again, nor would

[10] Quoted in Seumas MacManus, *The Story of the Irish Race* (New York: Devin-Adair Co., 1944), p. 607.

America. Those who survived to reassemble their lives on the two sides of the Atlantic were permanantly scarred by the experience of the famine years. In the future, they would organize their lives differently.

## THE SPLITTING OF THE CLANS

It may be only a thin line—almost a quirk of fate—that separates people of the same stock and sends them in different life directions. Anthropologists can sometimes trace the ancient choices which determined that half a tribe would take its migrating route to the west of a body of water, while the other half migrated eastward toward an entirely different future. For the Irish, even during the famine exodus, some such thin line of choice demarked the approximately one in seven who would decide on a life in America rather than in Ireland. In 1854, 16-year-old Mary of Skibbereen, County Cork, made such a choice. Her great granddaughter tells her story, as it has been passed down in the family.

> Mary, my great grandmother, was the oldest of seven children in a farming family in Cork. There was little work for anyone in Ireland then, and many of the young people were actually talking of leaving. Of course, the boys could help their fathers on the farms, but for girls the only future seemed to be bringing up babies and minding children. When Mary was 16, she decided to go to America, so her mother sent a letter to the only relative they had there at that time—a well-off cousin in New York—saying she wanted to send her eldest daughter. He sent passage money and promised to look after her when she arrived. It was a real adventure for a girl who had never been more than a few miles from home.
>
> Two months before her scheduled sailing date, a young friend of the family—also named Mary—who was ready to go to America, who had her ticket and her identification papers, lost the courage to leave. My great grandmother decided to take her place. She hurriedly packed her trunk, tied up her mother's best goosefeather tick, said goodby to her parents (whom she was never to see again) and boarded the little sailing ship for New York. It was such a bad crossing they were almost lost at sea. A month into the journey they ran into a severe storm that blew the ship 200 miles off course. The passengers were sick and frightened, and as they neared the coast of America the captain discovered he was nearer to Boston than New York. Since he had to put into port as soon as possible, he put into Boston.
>
> Here was Mary, alone in a strange country, in a city she had never heard of, carrying identification papers of another girl, and not knowing how she could get in touch with her relative in New York. But in those days there were "good women," as she called them, who went down to the ports to see that young girls coming in alone would come to no harm. Through them, Mary was placed in a well-to-do Boston Yankee home, where she worked from dawn till late in the evening for her board and 50 cents a week. Her employers invested her meager wages in their family shoe business, with the promise that she would receive payment in full upon her leaving, but when the family dismissed all boarders Mary never received her pay. She left to visit her sisters in nearby Andover, and it was there

> that she met and married Patrick, who had come from Ireland with his mother ten years before her, at the age of 12. In time their daughter married Michael, who had turned down the family farm to emigrate at the age of 21, and in time their daughter married my father. . . .[11]

So started an American line which is now dispersed from Massachusetts to California. Because Mary's childhood friend chose differently at the last moment, her line is in Ireland. In all likelihood, Mary considered neither her actions nor her life particularly noteworthy. We know relatively little about Mary's life in that well-to-do Boston Yankee home, nor do we know the details of Patrick's life, carrying cement to bricklayers on construction jobs as a young man, or serving with the Union Army under General Butler during the Civil War. We do know that as a married couple they prospered, for what is passed down in families tends to dwell on the daring and the successful; but unless Mary and Patrick were most unusual they did not consciously see themselves as part of the great Irish immigrant wave descending on American cities in the mid-1800s, nor did they ponder the effect they would have on American life. This was left to others of their own, and later, times to analyze.

## IRISH IMMIGRATION BEFORE 1830

There are no accurate figures for the total numbers of Irish immigrants who reached America before 1847, although the first census in 1790 showed 44,000 of Irish birth, with perhaps another 150,000 of Irish ancestry out of a total population of 4,000,000. Some historians contend that this figure was a gross underestimate of the total numbers, and that 33 percent or more of the population in 1776 was Irish-born or of Irish descent, but of more importance than the sheer numbers was the type of Irishman who had come during this early period, and the reasons that he failed to attract the attention as a distinct minority group that the later Irish received.

The majority of those Irish recorded in the first census lived south and west of Pennsylvania, and may have included more Irish Catholics than has commonly been supposed. In her recent study of Irish Catholic immigration between 1660 and 1775, Audrey Lockhart points out that many Catholics came as indentured servants to the southern colonies or as transported criminals who migrated from their original destination in the West Indies.[12] After winning release from their various forms of bondage, both groups tended to mingle and intermarry with Protestant Irish in those areas, like the South, where the Catholic Church was weak. Thus, because they started at the lowest social levels, and because they often ceased to be

[11] Fallows, private interview, 1975.

[12] Audrey Lockhart, *Some Aspects of Emigration from Ireland to the North American Colonies Between 1660 and 1775* (New York: Arno Press, 1976).

Catholic, they were slow in establishing distinctly Catholic Irish social institutions, and in achieving the upward mobility of the more numerous Ulster Protestant immigrant group.

In contrast to the Catholic Irish, the Protestant immigrants prior to 1830 were primarily small land-holders from Ulster in the northern part of Ireland, where the tradition of emigration had started in the 1700s and provided the bulk of the Protestant Irish who tended to gravitate to the frontiers just before and after the American Revolution. Although they were mainly Presbyterians who had been encouraged by the British government to come from Scotland as part of the Ulster "plantation" in the 1600s, these artisans and small farmers in northern Ireland had found they could no longer bear the burden of taxes, rents, and tithes brought on both by competition from large-scale agriculture and restrictions on the linen and woolen industry. As middle-class Protestants, they had not identified with the Catholic cause in Ireland, yet they did regard themselves as Irishmen since their forebears had lived in Ulster for over 100 years before their emigration.

Besides founding such settlements as Londonderry, New Hampshire, and starting Presbyterian churches in established Eastern communities, the Ulster immigrants had been among the first to pass through the settled coastal areas to make their homes in what was then the frontier. These were the pioneers who had located in the Blue Ridge region of Virginia as early as 1710, who had produced such a dense settlement in the lower Shenandoah Valley by 1743 that travelers' accounts of the time referred to it as the "Irish Tract," and whose descendants pushed with Daniel Boone into the Kentucky frontier in 1775.[13] Willing to bear the brunt of Indian attacks while less hardy settlers occupied the more protected lands, the Irish seemed almost the prototype of the rugged, freedom-loving frontiersman, anxious to break with the social conventions of the past.

James Leyburn, whose social analysis of frontier society has focused on the contribution of these early Irish toward the emergence of a new social order, has made it a point to warn, nevertheless, that:

> it would be a serious distortion of history to claim that the exodus from Ulster was a crusading search for freedom. On the contrary, all of the evidence shows that the people hoped to find social institutions in America very much like the ones they were leaving. These they did find, in the settled areas around their ports of debarkation. When they took farms in the wilderness they set to work forthwith to establish familiar institutions.[14]

The Irish did not conceive of a society unstructured by social class distinctions, but because of the improvisations required under frontier conditions

[13] Griffin, *The Irish in America,* p. 6.

[14] James G. Leyburn, *The Scotch-Irish* (Chapel Hill: University of North Carolina Press, 1962), p. 258.

they found themselves shifting the emphasis from distinctions based on ascription to those based on achievement. The role of the Ulstermen as frontiersmen, then, was that of helping to establish stratification patterns along more fluid lines than those they had known—fluid lines which came to be representative of the developing American society.

While their settlements east of the Appalachians marked, in Leyburn's view, "a turning point in American life," he concludes that the Irish:

> did not cause this social transformation; many deeply regretted it; but it was among them that the old standards of social class began to be eroded. No democratic theory attacked the old system. It was weakened by the fact that people by the thousands were constantly on the move. Stable social classes flourish only when residence is continuous in a community, so that men agree upon what brings prestige and position. . . . The mobility of the Scotch-Irish simply swept away all of these foundation stones of the class system for thousands of people.[15]

Although, as a group, the Irish immigrants prior to 1830 have sometimes been dismissed as having had no measurable impact on American life, it would perhaps be more accurate to say that the subsequent arrival of the far more numerous and culturally distinct Irish Catholics after 1830 simply obscured the impact of the earlier arrivals, who had been spatially and occupationally diversified, attuned to the prevailing institutions in the developing colonies, and overwhelmingly Protestant. Outside of New England, where the Irish were not always welcome (the General Court of Massachusetts in 1720 gave them seven months to leave the colony), little criticism attached to the group.[16]

Intermarriage with women of Irish background was not always possible, given the larger numbers of men during the early years of Irish migration, nor was it easy for the minority who were Catholic to maintain their ties with the Church, which was particularly weak in the South and in the frontier areas where so many of them had settled. For these reasons, many Irish immigrants prior to 1830 moved toward integration with the Anglo-American host society. They did not feel themselves particularly stigmatized as a minority ethnic group, and did not need to protect themselves from identification with their land of origin. They were known simply as Irishmen. By 1800, they had contributed not only frontiersmen for the western boundaries, but such prominent Americans as Jeremiah Smith who began the first paper factory at Dorchester, Massachusetts; Edward and William Patterson who started the manufacture of tinware at Berlin and New Britain, Connecticut; editors Hugh Gaine of the New York *Mercury* and John Dunlap of the *Pennsylvania Packet;* revolutionary heroes General Richard Montgomery and sharp-shooter Timothy Murphy; and

[15] Ibid., p. 266.
[16] Griffin, *The Irish in America,* p. 6.

signers of the Declaration of Independence such as Thomas Lynch, Edward Rutledge, and Charles Carroll.[17]

By the early 1800s, however, the situation had changed dramatically, as increasingly disastrous conditions in southern and western Ireland brought growing numbers of Catholic Irish who struggled to cope with their marginal status in a social order which the earlier Irish had helped to create. The simplest solution for those established Protestant Irish who sought to save themselves from identification with the more stigmatized new wave of immigrants was to "pass" into a more acceptable identity. The term Scotch-Irish was a social invention serving the purpose of setting social distance between themselves and the new wave of Catholic Irish, for whether they were originally of Scotch ancestry or not they were now identified as proper Protestant Americans.

While social history tends to focus on the trauma created by the later waves of Irish in the 1800s, it would be a mistake to overlook the presence of the Scotch-Irish who were already here. On the frontiers they had inadvertently contributed to the restructuring of American society along less ascriptive lines, and in many cities along the eastern seaboard they had established thriving Irish social organizations. They were sympathetic with the plight of the Irish remaining in Ireland, and ready to help reasonable numbers of Irish arriving in America. Yet, withal, many could not quite define the Catholic Irish as "their kind of people" in America, any more than they had defined them as "their kind of people" while they were still in Ireland.

In later years there would be outstanding leaders from the Protestant Irish community who would attempt to guide and help the later arrivals from the Catholic southern and western counties, but there would be others whose anxiety to proclaim themselves as proper Protestant Americans would contribute to violent clashes when the two groups met. It was not a foregone conclusion, by any means, that the presence of earlier Irish immigrants would markedly ease the way for the later arrivals, for they represented different social and religious backgrounds. To become Scotch-Irish was to signify this difference.

## IMMIGRATION AFTER 1830

After 1830, the composition and size of the Irish immigrant group altered radically. The combined impact of population increase and recurring crop failures in the 1830s swelled the estimated numbers arriving in American ports to over 200,000 for the single decade of the 1830s. During the decade of the 1840s the number rose again sharply to an estimated

[17] *Ibid.*, pp. 6–12.

800,000.[18] But since many Irish had left from English ports where no distinction was made between those of Irish and English background, it was not until 1847 when the Commissioners of Emigration in New York began recording the national origins of the two-thirds of immigrants entering through the port of New York that reliable figures became available. From 1847 through 1855 their figures show a cresting wave of Irish immigrants to New York, which began with 53,000 in 1847, swelled to 163,000 in 1851, and receded to 43,000 in 1885[19] (see Table 1). Compared with the other two largest immigrant groups of the time, the British and the Germans, the Irish presented the most agonizing adjustment for New York and other coastal cities where they disembarked. These were the "famine Irish."

*TABLE 1*

*NUMBERS (IN THOUSANDS) OF BRITISH, IRISH, AND GERMAN IMMIGRANTS TO NEW YORK, 1847–1855*

| | Year | | | | | | | | | |
|---|---|---|---|---|---|---|---|---|---|---|
| | 1847 | '48 | '49 | '50 | '51 | '52 | '53 | '54 | '55 | Total |
| British (English, Scottish, Welsh) | 12 | 31 | 39 | 37 | 38 | 42 | 35 | 37 | 28 | 299 |
| Irish | 53 | 91 | 112 | 117 | 163 | 118 | 113 | 82 | 43 | 892 |
| German | 53 | 52 | 56 | 46 | 70 | 119 | 120 | 177 | 53 | 746 |

Source: Terry Coleman, *Going to America* (N.Y.: Pantheon Books, a Division of Random House, 1972), Appendix C, p. 325.

As we have seen, the most severely affected by the potato blight were the Catholic subsistence farmers, who were as ill-prepared either for frontier or urban life as any immigrants who had come to America. It had taken real disaster at home to overcome their reluctance to leave Ireland, for most of them were people with deep roots in the familiar soil, and bound by the web of family and religious ties. The famine experience was, however, in Robert E. Kennedy's view, only "the final 'convincer' added to a set of conditions which encouraged emigration."[20] Kennedy's demographic analysis of Irish emigration patterns shows that only a small minority had actually been evicted—though the numbers were greater during famine years—but that emigration had become part of a general rural to urban population movement which "happened to cross international boundaries."[21]

Almost half the landholdings in Ireland in the early 1840s had been

[18] *Ibid.*, pp. 13–16.

[19] Terry Coleman, *Going to America* (N.Y.: Pantheon Books, 1972), Appendix C, p. 325.

[20] Robert E. Kennedy, Jr., *The Irish: Emigration, Marriage, and Fertility* (Berkeley: University of California Press, 1973), p. 43.

[21] *Ibid.*, p. 73.

below the desired size of five to fifteen acres that could be worked by one family using manual labor. Those with less than five acres were hardest hit by the famine, but as they were forced from the land the relative position of the average farmer declined too, and he became one of the new poor. After 1846, when the Corn Laws which had guaranteed preferential treatment for Irish grain on English markets were abolished, former tillage land was turned into pasture, the small ten-acre farm became less economical, and additional land could not be acquired by those who wanted to improve their situation. "The average farmer," Kennedy points out, "could achieve a higher standard of living only by giving up farming in Ireland."[22] Thus, for the young and adventurous, like 16-year-old Mary from County Cork, emigration was an exciting alternative to a bleak future; for others it was an act of desperation in order to survive; but for others still it was a recognition that they could only lose what little status and security they had if they remained in Ireland.

After a passage costing $12 to $15 for the six- to eight-week journey below decks on a crowded sailing vessel, many found the conditions on arrival little better than those they had left. Two immediate problems faced the authorities in ports along the Atlantic Seaboard: widespread disease among the debarking passengers and destitution among those who had already arrived. Quarantine stations were hastily set up to receive the sick, both in Canada and in the United States, with the most notorious stations located at Grosse Isle in the Saint Lawrence River and on Staten Island in New York harbor. In Canada, the arrival of the *Urania* from Cork on May 8, 1847, signaled the first of 84 plague-ridden ships that would sail up the Saint Lawrence in a single month. John Francis Maguire's eyewitness account, written in 1868, tells that "of the enormous number of vessels there was not one free from the taint of malignant typhus, the offspring of famine and of the foul ship-hold. This fleet of vessels literally reeked with pestilence."[23] Taken by surprise, the Canadian authorities hastily shunted the fever victims to Grosse Isle—sometimes literally heaving them onto the beaches to make their way toward the overcrowded fever sheds as best they could. In New York, the Staten Island Quarantine Station was similarly overwhelmed by the hundred and more diseased immigrants arriving on each ship. In 1847 and 1848, the majority of those arriving were either sick or destitute, or both, having brought few resources to make a start in the new country.

In an effort to bring some control to the situation, the New York Commissioners of Emigration had imposed, in 1847, a payment of $1.50 for each immigrant: to help pay for quarantine, find jobs, and reimburse the counties if they became public charges. Such measures scarcely touched the problem. An alarmed Congress in the same year passed severe Passenger

[22] *Ibid.,* p. 88.
[23] John Francis Maguire, *The Irish in America* (New York: Arno Press, 1969), p. 135.

Acts, ostensibly with the humanitarian purpose of reducing the numbers that greedy shipowners could crowd on their vessels, but with the secondary aim of reducing the total immigration. Even though all manner of ill-equipped ships had been called into service for the human traffic from Irish and British ports, prices for the passage soared, and the fare to New York doubled. Boston resurrected and enforced an 1837 law requiring a $1,000 bond from the shipmaster as a guarantee that the aged, infirm, and poor would not become public charges for ten years.[24] And still they came.

Since it was widely believed at the time that Britain was, as a matter of policy, deporting Irish convicts and paupers to the United States in order to be rid of them, attempts to limit access to American ports were viewed as justified. British Canada, it was felt, should and could take in the arrivals. The British government, in fact, was already stung by criticism of its callousness toward the Irish during the famine and could scarcely have risked calling attention to the problem by officially encouraging Irish emigration to the United States. Even landlords in Ireland, anxious to consolidate their estates by "shoveling out" their tenants, sometimes offered them cheap passage to Canada while speaking righteously of providing colonists for British North America. Since settlers really were needed in Canada, enticements were made available in the form of extremely low fares, and many destitute famine victims took advantage of the situation with the intent of migrating south to the United States—legally or illegally—as soon as the opportunity arose.

A special aura attached to America which Canada simply did not share: America had violently broken the tie with Britain. Conor Cruise O'Brien describes the feeling of many Irish:

> The same people who had oppressed America were still oppressing Ireland. So an Irishman could be a patriotic American: perhaps a more patriotic American than many other Americans. Immigrant children of other stocks might hear about the American revolution without much emotion. But to an Irish boy, in the mid-nineteenth century, the American revolution, 'freeing the country from the British,' genuinely sounded good. Many a successful political career must have grown from the seed of that first sincere, spontaneous identification.[25]

Irish enthusiasm to identify with the American cause, however, was not matched by American enthusiasm for the arriving Irish. Indeed, the Irish hatred for the British appeared less a virtue than a fanaticism to Americans who were Anglo-Saxon in so many ways, and for whom Anglo conformity was the dominant expectation for incoming immigrants.

In Eastern cities where the famine immigrants debarked, even those ideologically liberal Anglo-Americans who had been sympathetic and gen-

[24] Coleman, *Going to America,* p. 139.
[25] Conor Cruise O'Brien, *States of Ireland* (New York: Pantheon Books, 1972), p. 44.

erous in their contributions for famine victims in Ireland were alarmed by the destitution, the aggressiveness, and the rising crime rates which seemed to characterize this newest, largest, and most unwelcome immigrant group. Although the social climate and capacity for absorbing the influx of Irish varied from one city to another, the immigrants themselves displayed enough characteristics in common so that Anglo-Americans were quick to stereotype the newcomers negatively in terms of an "Irish personality" or "Irish character." Even though the characteristics were largely traceable to similar socioeconomic backgrounds, a common religious experience, and shared trauma, the thinking of the time tended to interpret them as permanent racial endowments and to question whether any group so different could adapt to American life.

The inheritance of these Catholic Irish included scars from centuries of social and religious subjugation in Ireland, the memory of famine years which had virtually destroyed the familiar social fabric of their lives, and a consequent passion for freedom which they hoped that America, having so recently fought for its own freedom, might satisfy. But it was also an inheritance of rural ways that were ill-adapted to the urban centers where the majority of the Irish began their new lives and of a defensive peasant Catholicism that soon antagonized other American Catholics as well as the Protestant majority. Moreover, those Irishmen who had preceded them in smaller numbers during the previous century had come largely from a different part of Ireland, from a different social background, and from a different religious experience. As the numbers of famine immigrants grew, it became apparent that the relations between the two Irish groups would not be universally cordial.

Given the inheritance they had brought with them, and the stereotypes that quickly formed to set them apart from the Anglo-American host society, it was clear that the adjustment of the Catholic Irish of the famine years would be unlike that of any previous immigrant group and that the conditions were scarcely auspicious for mutual understanding or easy assimilation. Although it soon became apparent that these Irish would become the first large group of immigrants who, for economic and social reasons, were to turn away from the rural westward frontier, it was equally apparent that they would have to be pioneers of another kind. In spite of their rural inheritance, it would be they who would settle and leave their distinctive stamp on the growing American cities in the decades to come.

# CHAPTER THREE

# Early Years in America

After centuries of life as rural peasants who had cherished and passed on their bit of land from generation to generation, the famine Irish had finally turned away from the land. Taming an American frontier was not the kind of farming they had been accustomed to, and besides they had no resources for getting to the frontier. Nor could very many afford established farms in gentler areas. The sociability of the Irish crossroads hamlet could not be duplicated except where there were other Irishmen with whom to share their lives. For these reasons, and because the industrial expansion of mid-nineteenth-century American cities offered unskilled, if low paying, jobs, the Irish became an urban people in America. The transition was not an easy one. William Shannon has called it "a journey from one edge of the continuum of social organization to the other."[1]

American cities at that time had scarcely learned to cope with themselves, much less to cope with a sudden influx of unskilled immigrants. Only 15 percent of Americans lived in cities in the 1850s—an even smaller percentage than the 20 percent of urban dwellers in Ireland—but for the rural Irish who emigrated to America, cities offered the only way they saw to improve their social and economic positions.[2] As many as forty immigrants were crowded into a single cellar space in the developing slums of Boston and New York where the most destitute lived, and where their death rates were virtually as high as they had been in Irish rural areas during the famine.[3] Assaults on police officers and other forms of violence soared. Although much of the crime was the petty crime of the desperately poor, this was a day when clear distinctions were made between the deserving and the undeserving poor, and the Irish clearly did not possess the traits that Protestant Americans associated with the deserving. Although many had been forced to take menial jobs in order to live, they had learned from experience that the meek were not the survivors of the famine and the humble were not the ones who adjusted best to life in America. Indeed, as the Irish were quick to observe, it was not the sociable

[1] Introduction to Dennis Clark, *The Irish in Philadelphia: Ten Generations of Urban Experience* (Philadelphia: Temple University Press, 1974), p. xiv.

[2] Kennedy, Robert E. Jr., *The Irish: Emigration, Marriage, and Fertility* (Berkeley: University of California Press, 1973), p. 82.

[3] *Ibid.*, p. 51.

virtues of the countryman—his distrust of wealth, his fatalism in defeat, his loyalties to the family—that marked the successful man in urban America. Whether defined as deserving or not by Anglo-Americans, the immigrants had not suffered so long or traveled so far only to succumb now.

Irish men took the unskilled, risky jobs that others did not want. In addition to their reputations as hard workers they acquired reputations as tough fighters and hard drinkers. Men who hauled concrete, dug canals, laid railroads, and raised buildings also raised the pint of beer, and, in Puritan eyes, raised an unacceptable amount of hell afterwards. Having lived under oppressive conditions in Ireland for so long, they had acquired a tolerance for violence and violent methods which, though forbidden by the Catholic Church, had often been the only perceived recourse for injustice. Compounding this tolerance for violence—harking back to the examples of sporadic terror provided by roving gangs like the Whiteboys of Munster or the Terry Alts in Clare in retaliation for intolerable exploitation—was the necessity to conform outwardly to the prevailing standards in order to survive economically. The inner tensions set up by such conformity had been somewhat relieved in Ireland by religious faith and strong social bonds, but where these were weakened in America, men were no longer held by the gentle social pressures of the traditional male gatherings in a rural home or village shebeen, and drinking often broke the bounds of civility to become a disorderly escape from tension.

With the more prosperous and able-bodied Irish immigrants tending to disperse throughout the country, while the destitute and helpless remained close to their ports of debarkation, the 1860 Census showed that the majority of the 1,611,000 Irish in America had remained in New England, New Jersey, New York, and Pennsylvania, and nearly two-thirds were unskilled.[4] Partly as a result of being able to draw quickly on a pool of unskilled labor from among their fellow Irishmen, the more enterprising moved into construction work or became recruiting agents for American companies. Others became bondsmen, collecting commissions on the sale of railroad and shipping tickets, arranging rentals in boarding houses, and profiting from both employers and immigrants.

Perhaps most notable among the Irish was their awareness of the uses of power. In Ireland, politics had been a struggle to be waged by any available means. Because their familiarity with the language proved an early advantage, Irishmen found they could begin in America where they had left off in Ireland, and with 43 percent of the entire foreign-born population of the United States in 1850 of Irish origin, their politicians could draw on a sizable body of support.[5] At a time when social services for the poor were largely private or nonexistent, Irish politicians provided stop-gap re-

[4] Maldwyn Allen Jones, *American Immigration* (Chicago: University of Chicago Press, 1960), p. 118.

[5] Carl Wittke, *The Irish in America* (New York: Russell and Russell, 1970), p. 24.

lief for the destitute in exchange for their loyalty at the polls, for, as Carl Wittke observes: "Irish peasants had been tools of their landlords; it was not very different to become tools of political bosses, who marched them in groups to the polls and cemented the allegiance with free liquor."[6] Not only did the extraordinary Irish need for sociability and interaction with others provide a natural arena for political skills which would later dominate urban politics, but in the transition from the subordinate position of a lower caste in Ireland to the competitive position they intended to occupy in America, the political arena provided the most direct route. Daniel Bell points out that if competition between plural groups takes place largely in the political arena, it is for the simple reason that status competition is diffuse and economic competition is dispersed between interests and occupations; however, political competition is direct and tangible, with rewards specified through legislation or by the direct allocation of jobs and privileges.[7] So it was for the Irish.

Irish women, who increasingly came in equal numbers with the men, acquired a somewhat different image. Like Mary from Cork, who worked for a well-to-do Boston family for her board and 50 cents a week in 1845, thousands of other young country girls became domestics at a time when even Anglo-Americans who were not well-to-do had a live-in girl to help with the housework. Although young Irish women had experienced extreme male dominance in Ireland, they were as free as their brothers to migrate from rural homes. Being English-speaking and single, they could hope to improve their social position and in all likelihood find a husband in America—neither of which was easy to accomplish in post-famine Ireland.[8] From their earnings the women, like the men, saved to "bring out" the families from Ireland, arranging for jobs or lodgings as their brothers, sisters, cousins, or parents joined them in America. The Irish Immigrant Society of New York was only one of many organizations that would arrange passage through its Irish offices, and between 1848 and 1900 at least 260 million dollars in "America money" went from America to Ireland to pay for passage tickets or to help with the rent and improve the standard of living for those who remained in Ireland.[9] Although advertisements for domestic help frequently specified that only Protestants would be acceptable—a variation on the "No Irish Need Apply" notices—Irish women were in demand as domestics and were in a position to observe such gentle manners and social graces as their employers might display, thus speeding their adaptation to American ways.

For both men and women, the Catholic Church served as a continu-

[6] *Ibid.*, pp. 103–4.

[7] Daniel Bell, "Ethnicity and Social Change," in Nathan Glazer and Daniel P. Moynihan (Eds.), *Ethnicity: Theory and Experience* (Cambridge: Harvard University Press, 1975), p. 161.

[8] Kennedy, *The Irish*, pp. 84–85.

[9] *Ibid.*, p. 22.

ing thread helping to bind their present strivings and future hopes to a common past in the Irish village. Their priests, fellow sufferers during the long years of English oppression, also emigrated in significant numbers. Prior to the arrival of the famine immigrants, the Catholic Church in America had been moving toward accommodation with American culture and ways. Yet despite these tendencies and the influence of large numbers of German Catholic immigrants, who viewed themselves as intellectually better suited to lead American Catholicism, the Irish succeeded by force of numbers in establishing a predominantly Irish institution.[10] Where so little else brought prestige and a feeling of success, the ability to contribute toward building a handsome church—bringing the true religion to America—was viewed with pride. The donations of desperately poor people raised the first Catholic churches in many communities; the Irish men built them; and if they were uneasy unless the priest was also Irish, it was because their sense of Irishness and their Catholicism were so intertwined.

These, then, were some of the shared characteristics with which the famine Irish approached American life: a deliberate choice to leave a rural past behind; a manner of behaving frequently interpreted as troublesome aggressiveness, ill-suited to their impoverished condition as new arrivals; a willingness to take the unskilled jobs that were available while moving into business and politics as the opportunity arose; a familiarity with the social ways of the well-to-do through their women; and a concern for the development of an Irish Catholic church which would link them with the old life. If we add to these characteristics the general youthfulness of the immigrants, the nearly equal numbers of men and women, the gregariousness and sociability characteristic of neighborhoods constantly replenished by new arrivals from Ireland, and their practical approach to the uses of political power which allowed them to provide social services not available through any other means, we have some of the basic ingredients with which the Irish functioned in urban settings.

## IRISH RECEPTION IN FOUR COMMUNITIES

Anglo-Americans who formed stereotypes of the "typical Irishman" based on their perceptions of the famine immigrants failed to recognize that not all the Irish were impoverished, unskilled, tolerant of violence, politically conscious, or even Catholic. But it is true, nonetheless, that the famine Irish were among the most homogeneous of those who left Ireland, and their hopes for socioeconomic betterment had to be viewed in the context of deeply ingrained norms of a rural peasant society which they did not consciously set out to change. Yet change did occur. It may be that in later

[10] John Cogley, *Catholic America* (New York: The Dial Press, 1973), Ch. 2.

years, when there was more choice in the matter, those who held most strongly to the normative ideals of rural Ireland simply did not emigrate. But for the famine Irish—most of whom would not have left voluntarily if they had not been driven to it—the change in style and character would seem to be more the result of being thrown into American society with its different kind of social structure.

Since social structure is also a variable—affected by region, community size, social composition of the population, and stage of economic development—it follows that even such a homogeneous group as the famine immigrants would experience life differently in different types of communities. Although some Irish immigrants found their way to every state of the Union, the vast majority stayed close to the eastern seaboard. In the section that follows we will consider briefly how they fared in their initial contacts with Americans in each of four Eastern communities.

In the decade of the 1840s, which marked the first significant confrontation of the famine Irish with American life, New York City, with 350,000 people, was already a competitive, wealthy, and heterogeneous city with a large Irish Protestant community, among whom figured professional men, merchants, and established Irish politicians.[11] Philadelphia, with over 220,000 people, was just entering a period of burgeoning growth in industry, transportation, and commerce, with room for physical expansion, openings for new workers, and existing Irish social organizations.[12] Boston was at that time a tightly knit commercial town of 85,000 people, with limited resources, an aristocratic leadership, and a bustling port through which countless immigrants had already passed on their way to more promising places.[13] Stamford, Connecticut, was a quiet village of 3,500 people, governed by a coterie of Yankee leaders and facing a period of apparent stagnancy or decline.[14]

On the face of it, any immigrant with choice in the matter and advance knowledge of these few facts might have headed for Philadelphia as the place most likely to offer a chance for both sociability and advancement. But these facts were not known, and scarcely any of the famine Irish had a choice in the matter. They were fleeing Ireland rather than embrac-

[11] Sources dealing with the Irish in New York during this period include Carl Wittke, *The Irish in America;* John Francis Maguire, *The Irish in America* (New York: Arno Press, 1969); Nathan Glazer and Daniel P. Moynihan, *Beyond the Melting Pot* rev. ed., (Cambridge: MIT Press, 1970), pp. 217–87; Stephen Birmingham, *Real Lace: America's Irish Rich* (New York: Harper & Row, 1973); William Shannon, *The American Irish* (New York: Macmillan, 1963).

[12] The most complete source dealing with Philadelphia during this period is Dennis Clark's *The Irish in Philadelphia.*

[13] Sources dealing with the Irish in Boston during this period include Oscar Handlin, *Boston's Immigrants* (Cambridge: Harvard University Press, 1959); Shannon, *The American Irish,* Ch. 17; Wittke, *The Irish in America,* Ch. 3.

[14] The most complete source dealing with Stamford during this period is Estelle F. Feinstein, *Stamford in the Gilded Age,* (Stamford: The Stamford Historical Society, 1973).

ing a future for which they had planned. Except that some already had kin in a particular city where they would be met, almost any American port would do. The majority landing in Eastern ports came to New York or Boston; very few came by direct immigration from Ireland to Philadelphia; none came directly to Stamford. In theory, since they were disproportionately young and mobile, they could drift toward the areas where jobs were available and would eventually find the best locations. Indeed, at mid-nineteenth century, it was quite common for half of the working population of any community to have moved between one census and the next, and many of these might have been Irish. Yet movement of this kind required, then as now, enough financial and social flexibility to make choices and to take advantage of opportunities, as well as some knowledge of what those opportunities were. Arriving in large numbers and with few resources, many of the famine immigrants simply remained near the ports where they had landed. Their subsequent perception of American society derived largely from their limited interaction with Americans in that specific locale.

### New York

Between 1845 and 1855 close to one million Irish, most of whom had never before traveled more than a few miles from their birthplaces in rural Ireland, arrived in New York City. The Irish Emigrant Society, founded in 1814, had been attempting to provide free advice to new arrivals to protect them from exploitation by swindlers and boarding-house keepers, and to give advice on traveling inland and establishing themselves in America, but the sudden influx of destitute famine Irish was more than it was equipped to handle. While New York City was merely a port of entry for many, it became home for thousands. By 1855, the Irish-born made up 28 percent of the city's population and 34 percent of its voters. Already a thriving metropolis, within five years New York was also the "largest Irish city in the world" with over 203,000 Irish-born out of a total population of 806,000. Neighboring Brooklyn accounted for another 57,000 Irish-born in its total population of 267,000.[15]

New York was, however, quite accustomed to receiving newcomers. Even the arrival of the famine Irish in enormous numbers was viewed more as a temporary disruption than as a catastrophic event. Within a few years of the peak Irish immigration to New York in 1851 the German immigrants arrived in nearly equal numbers.[16] That the resources of the city were strained was apparent from the lack of adequate housing, as basements and dugouts under cellar floors became homes for the more destitute arrivals.

[15] William D. Griffin, *The Irish in America: A Chronology and Fact Book* (Dobbs Ferry, N.Y.: Oceana Publications, Inc., 1972), p. 17.

[16] See Table 1, p. 23.

Disease raised the death rate among the Irish to 21 per 1,000—nearly twice that of the Philadelphia Irish.[17] Competition for jobs brought out the "No Irish Need Apply" signs; the Paddy wagons lurched off to local jails with drunken and rowdy Irish (*Padraic* or Patrick) passengers. The leaders of the predominantly Protestant Irish community watched tensely as the incoming peasants disregarded their leadership and engaged in bar fights and street crime.

John Francis Maguire, who reported in 1868 on what he had observed during his travels among the Irish in America, spoke of "the evil of remaining in the great cities" and described in lurid detail the overcrowding, misery, and unsanitary conditions among the immigrants who had settled in New York. Feeling that the Irish were courting disaster by adopting an urban life style for which they were unprepared, he wrote:

> It is easy enough to explain why and how those who should not have remained in the great cities did so; but it is not so easy to depict the evils which have flowed, which daily flow, which, unhappily for the race, must continue to flow from the pernicious tendency of the Irish peasant to adopt a mode of livelihood for which he is not suited by previous knowledge or training, and to place himself in a position dangerous to his morals, if not fatal to his independence.[18]

In the decade of the 1850s, healthy Irish immigrants could work as laborers for 75 cents a day, and healthy girls could receive room and board and $1.00 a week as housemaids. Although 21 percent of the national labor force was in unskilled occupations at that time, and among immigrants generally the percent rose to 35, it was still higher among the Irish. In New York, 25 percent of the Irish working population was composed of laborers, carters, porters, and waiters, with another 25 percent in domestic service and 10 percent in the garment trade operating newly invented sewing machines.[19] This put at least 50 percent at the lowest rung of the occupational ladder. In the same decade, 55 percent of those arrested for crime in New York City were Irish-born,[20] yet 25 percent of the police arresting them were also Irish.[21] Concentration of Irish in slum areas had already become apparent as early as the 1830s, especially in the area known as Five Points. From here the extent of Irish settlement gradually spread during the next generation until it included the entire Lower East Side as far north as the Fourteenth Ward and as far east as the Seventh.[22]

Yet, as Daniel Patrick Moynihan has pointed out:

[17] Clark, *The Irish in Philadelphia,* p. x.
[18] Maguire, *The Irish in America,* pp. 216–17.
[19] Jones, *American Immigration,* p. 130.
[20] *Ibid.,* p. 133.
[21] Griffin, *The Irish in America,* p. 17.
[22] Jones, *American Immigration,* p. 134.

> the basic patterns of Irish life in New York had been set. The hordes that arrived at mid-century strengthened some of these patterns more than others, but they did not change them nearly so much as they were changed by them. They got off the boat to find their identity waiting for them: they were to be Irish-Catholic Democrats.[23]

The leadership of Tammany Hall, the Democratic Party's urban council, had been wrested from Anglo-American hands in the 1840s, and ushered in an era of Irish domination of New York political life that continued into the twentieth century. With over one-third of the voters of New York Irish-born, their political power was substantial, and nativist nightmares about the strength of the "Irish vote" could hardly be written off as a figment of the imagination.

But if the Irish were politically and socially conspicuous, they were scarcely the first or only immigrant group with which the city had to contend. The German immigrants had arrived almost simultaneously, and in nearly equal numbers, and together the Irish and Germans made up 44 percent of the city's population in 1855.[24] By the 1880s, when the children of the famine immigrants had reached maturity, Jews and Italians were beginning to pour into New York; by then, the Irish were firmly in command of the political power of the city and in a position to think of themselves as old hands in America. The pace of urban growth and change was such that resentments were dispersed, coalitions formed and reformed, and the city reeled on with the Irish now part of its mosaic pattern. Meanwhile, through New York City passed countless other Irishmen on their way to villages and towns of the surrounding area and across the Midwest to the Pacific.

### Philadelphia

Six generations of Irish immigrants had settled in Philadelphia prior to the 1840s, but nothing had fully prepared the city for the seventh generation—the famine Irish. In his study of ten generations of Irish in Philadelphia, Dennis Clark observes that it was this seventh generation which would "greatly change Philadelphia's composition and its posture with respect to immigrants."[25] Because Philadelphia did not receive the direct impact of newly landed immigrants that the port cities of Boston and New York did, its percentage of Irish-born was consistently lower. At mid-century, the Irish-born constituted 21 percent of Philadelphia's population—about 72,000 Irish in a city which had grown from 220,000 to 340,000 in the previous decade, and which was just then entering a rapid expansionary phase of its growth.

Already a broad-based industrial center, a thriving port, and the hub

[23] Glazer and Moynihan, *Beyond the Melting Pot,* p. 221.
[24] *Ibid.,* p. 8.
[25] Clark, *The Irish in Philadelphia,* p. 24.

of an expanding rail network, Philadelphia was also known for the quality of its education, the extent of its charitable work, and its support of the arts. Clark sums up Philadelphia's feeling about itself in these words:

> To the upper class and the comfortable middle class of the city, what had been created was good. They looked askance at New York and accorded Boston grudging recognition. The exciting and profitable economic development of Philadelphia was a source of pride. It was sufficiently rewarding and diverting that the Irish immigration, though at first considered menacing, did not on second thought appear to pose a major threat. Indeed, the labor supplied by the immigrants was essential. They were a valuable pool of laborers and servants for a city intent on industrial greatness and residential enjoyment.[26]

Those arriving in Philadelphia were primarily young and single persons who had disembarked in New York. Philadelphia was not without its tensions during those years, as violent conflicts erupted early in the 1840s between Irish newcomers and nativists. Church burnings and Know-Nothing riots reflected the Protestant native's growing fear of Catholicism and of competition for jobs at the lower occupational levels. Newspapers reinforced the stereotyped image of the Catholic immigrants as socially troublesome and inferior—a lower order of mankind. As in other cities, the Irish responded by creating their own separate organizations, banding together in ethnic neighborhoods, and remaining semi-aloof from the Philadelphians who needed them economically but did not accept them socially.

At the same time, both natives and newcomers were caught up in the excitement of an expanding city. Peasants starved for property in Ireland found that they could become property owners in Philadelphia, where a two-story house was within the range of possibility for a thrifty workingman and where home ownership became a common pattern unknown to New York or Boston Irishmen. Where loans were difficult to get, Irish building and loan associations developed as people's banks—often as adjuncts to Catholic churches, fraternal organizations, and Irish neighborhood and workingmen's groups—to finance home ownership and encourage thrift and family improvement. Those who eventually prospered as bankers, lawyers, physicians, editors, politicians, and the like found they could move into more prestigious middle- and upper-class neighborhoods. Although the majority of the famine immigrants were at first concentrated in slum areas, their arrival coincided with a boom in residential building such that within a short time even in the less desirable areas up to half of the property owners were Irish, living in "tidy row houses on an orderly city street." By comparison with the conditions they had known, the immigrants were able to aspire to, or were already living in, unbelievable affluence and security. Even the death rate for Philadelphia Irish, at 12 per 1,000, was little more than half that of New York, and only one-third that

[26] *Ibid.*, pp. 33–34.

of Boston, reflecting not only the hardiness of those who found their way to Philadelphia but also the less crowded and disease-infested living conditions.

Irish fraternal organizations were already established in Philadelphia by the time the famine Irish arrived, and these proliferated with the social needs of the newcomers for interaction and mutual aid. The Friendly Sons of Saint Patrick—founded in 1771 and later combined with the Hibernian Society for the Relief of Emigrants from Ireland—included both Protestant and Catholic Irish. Irish military and fire brigades provided what Clark has called:

> a medium for association, celebration, and nationalistic activity. They were based partly upon nostalgia for the old country and a concern for its welfare and partly on the need for ethnic solidarity and interaction. . . . They were also channels for business or political advancement, and an arena for the exercise of personal influence or the assertion of social status.[27]

Less socially acceptable, but still serving as rallying places for ethnic interests, were secret organizations like the Fenian Brotherhood dedicated to Irish independence, or even the gangs of Irish hoodlums who roamed the neighborhoods. And above all, the Catholic parish organizations and the neighborhood saloons—both of them anathema to the native Protestants—were two transplanted institutions which reached all levels of the Irish community with their own special versions of counsel, guidance, and camaraderie.

Philadelphia, at mid-century, proved able to include the Irish in its vision of the future. Troublesome as they might appear, stereotyped as they might be in the imagination, they did not prove to be a serious threat. What Philadelphia was in a position to offer was exactly what the famine Irish most desired: diversification in jobs which started at the unskilled level but which could offer advancement for the enterprising, decent housing, and association with others who shared a sense of ethnic identity. Because the proportion of Irish-born to native Americans was lower than in New York or Boston, and because the Irish in Philadelphia were active in, but never controlled, the politicial life of the city, they were finally able to move in steady steps toward the respectability they craved—respectability both within their own ethnic subsociety and in the eyes of the larger Philadelphia.

### Boston

Prior to 1845, Boston had served merely as a port of debarkation, but Boston's Irish immigrants stayed and by 1850 made up 31 percent of the city's population. Since 75 percent were unskilled, the ready supply of cheap labor attracted construction bosses, who advertised for as many as 2,000

[27] *Ibid.*, pp. 110–11.

men for unskilled work elsewhere—work that Anglo-Americans disdained. Leaving women and children behind in Boston, these men departed for the job of building roads, canals, and railroads in distant places. Nearer the city, mechanization in textiles and shoes led to the hiring of other Irishmen to do work previously done by native girls, while in the city itself about 65 percent of Boston's Irish working population in 1850 was engaged in public works, as stevedores at the wharfs, or as yard and house servants.[28] Because the Irish provided much-needed labor for the rapid industrial expansion that had just begun, they were tolerated by the Boston leadership.

Oscar Handlin, in his classic study of Boston's immigrants, describes the despair of the Irish who could no longer turn to their gardens, their pigs, their chickens to help them eke out a subsistence living. All must be purchased in the city from wages providing less than the price of food. At best, "the Irish remained but shabbily equipped to meet the multifarious problems imposed on them by urban life."[29] South Boston emerged as an urban slum, a congested and frightening district soon deserted by native Americans. Crime soared by as much as 400 percent, and the death rate among the Irish climbed to 37 per 1,000—three times that of Philadelphia.

Unable to spread out because of the physical layout of the city, the Irish became an ingrown group surrounded by hostility. Handlin describes the "inability of the native-born to understand the ideas of their new neighbors," a mental set that perpetuated social segregation and led to a growing fear among Bostonians that the Irish could never be assimilated.[30] To the Irish it seemed that Bostonians were tolerant and helpful to all but them. The reform movements which caught the interest of ideologically liberal Bostonians—especially the abolition movement—were unattractive and threatening to the Irish. Accustomed to viewing dramatic social change as better left in the hands of God than tampered with at the secular level, they were particularly distressed at the prospect of having to compete for a marginal existence with freed slaves. In Boston, blacks were already in a more fortunate position than were the Irish themselves. Nor did increased contact with Bostonians lead to better understanding, but instead, Handlin concludes that such contact

> bred conflict rather than reconciliation. Irish Catholics could not think like their neighbors without a complete change in way of life. And natives could adopt no aspect of Catholic ideas without passing through a radical intellectual revolution.[31]

Constant replenishment of the Irish community through continued immigration, plus constant rediscovery that they were viewed with disdain

[28] Wittke, *The Irish in America,* p. 26.
[29] Handlin, *Boston's Immigrants,* pp. 86–87.
[30] *Ibid.,* p. 185.
[31] *Ibid.,* p. 149.

in Boston, served to strengthen the cohesiveness of the group and to make necessary the development of a separate institutional life. The Catholic Church provided consolation, familiar forms, and comforting truths in an environment whose social forces were little understood. For example, the growing effort of Bostonians to enforce compulsory education in common schools with a distinctly Protestant cast was met with a resistance whose own cry for a separate Catholic school system was equally vociferous.

When the latent political strength of the Irish was finally mobilized, the surge in voter strength ended whatever limited tolerance the Bostonians had felt toward the Irish in the past, and triggered a reaction in the nativist movement which sought to restrict Irish rights and privileges—including extension of the five-year residency requirement for voting to twenty-one years! Social and political antagonisms recurrently took the form of confrontations between Irish and Boston Yankees, for during the forty-year period following the famine influx no other ethnic groups came in sizable enough numbers to dilute the impact of the Irish.

In the midst of this tension, the Civil War broke out. The Irish figured prominently in bloody draft riots which broke out in New York to protest the provision allowing men to escape service by providing a substitute or paying a $300 fee. For the Irish, conscription was particularly objectionable since it came almost simultaneously with emancipation and required the Irishman to fight for his Negro competitor in the labor market. Yet despite the opposition to the draft that appeared in a number of cities including Boston, documents reveal that between 150,000 and 170,000 Irish-born Americans were taking part in the Union cause.[32] Considering the second- and third-generation Irish who also served, the Irish contribution actually went beyond their proportion in the population. Like the Germans, the Irish demanded and were given separate Hibernian units, and it was with some amazement that Bostonians who had believed the Irish to be hopeless in their opposition to Lincoln, in their support of slavery, the Democratic Party, and the South, and in their resistance to any kind of reform now watched as the Irish enlisted. Previously distrustful of the motives of the abolitionists in the North, the Irish now defined the South as the revolutionary side which threatened the lawfully established government through its attempt to secede.

For their part, the Bostonians finally recognized that the Irish in their midst were there to stay, were an overwhelming political force, and were giving a distinctly Irish cast to their community. By 1885, the children of Irish parents outnumbered the children of older stock in Boston, and the city had become predominantly Irish. In time, the surge of development which had been built on a base of cheap Irish labor lost its dynamism as the Irish attained skills and power, and Boston's industrial leadership gave way to other cities where the bitterness of prolonged hostility between two antagonistic cultures had not drained them of a broader vision of the future.

[32] Wittke, *The Irish in America,* Ch. 13.

## Stamford

Before the completion of the New York-New Haven railroad line in 1848, Stamford, Connecticut, was a quiet town with a population under 4,000, most of whom were well established Yankees. The completion of the railroad put Stamford within easy traveling distance of both New York and New Haven and brought with it hundreds of newly arrived Irish immigrants looking for work in Stamford's rapidly expanding industries. By 1850 the population had expanded to 5,200 and a decade later passed the 7,000 mark. By 1870, 28 percent of the adult males in the community were Irish-born[33]—the first non-English, non-Protestant, non-Yankee settlers to have entered the conservative town. In her social analysis of Stamford's development between 1868 and 1893, Estelle Feinstein has documented Stamford's attempts to cope with the unfamiliar stresses occasioned by this clearly alien group.

Distinct Irish sections emerged in the town as the new arrivals clustered first near the railroad roundhouse in a section called Dublin, then expanded to Kerrytown across the Mill River, flowing into blocks of apartments and multi-family houses put up by local contractors expressly for the Irish element—with kitchens in the basements and rooms to let upstairs. The town's reaction was distinctly uneasy. The Irish were equated in the local weekly journals with brawny, untutored laborers at best, and with drunkards and cursing street brawlers at worst. Town prohibition laws enacted in the 1870s, as well as regular raids on Lee's, McDevitt's and Mulligan's saloons in the years just prior to the ordinances, symbolized Yankee displeasure with Irish ways. Yet, occupationally, the overwhelmingly unskilled Irish men presented no competition to the native Americans, and over half of the Irish were women and girls who easily found work as domestics.

Arriving Irish families, and those formed through marriages of the young unmarried immigrants, swelled the number of school-age children until crowding presented a crisis which some natives hoped to resolve through consolidation of the existing district schools. Although a Catholic elementary school had been established in the Dublin neighborhood, and the majority of those in Dublin's district school were also Irish, over 25 percent of the Irish children attended no school at all. Efforts to expand the schools through consolidation, however, met with hostility both from Irish parents, who wanted to keep their neighborhood school and who were deeply offended by the requirement of daily Bible reading from the King James version, and from Yankee parents, who disliked and feared the Irish children. By the time a new school was finally built in 1877, the parochial school had taken matters into its own hands by establishing a convent for a Catholic teaching order. In her analysis of Stamford's development during this period, Feinstein concludes that

[33] Since Stamford attracted more women than men, the actual percentage of Irish would have been higher than 28 percent.

> because of the failures to construct a public school house in Dublin, consolidation of the schools had temporarily restricted opportunities for Catholic children to acquire public education in their own neighborhood and promoted the growth of an alternative Catholic system.[34]

Meanwhile, the highly visible and alien Irish Catholic minority provoked continuing resentments which mirrored the tensions prevalent in so many other small New England industrial towns trying to assimilate various cultural minorities. John Higham, describing the tensions in such small towns, writes that:

> an Irishman's loyalty to his priest was too firm for anxious Protestants to rest easily. And along with the religious distrust went social criticism. Americans pictured the Irish as rowdy ne'er-do-wells, impulsive, quarrelsome, drunken, and threadbare. Childhood conflicts gave these attitudes deep and early roots in many minds, for middle-class boys growing up in the American towns of the late nineteenth century battled incessantly with roughneck Irish gangs from the other side of the tracks.[35]

The view from the other side of the tracks, where the Irish lived, is given more simply by a first-generation Irishman recalling his childhood during this era:

> There's quite a tradition woven around this (Irish) section of the city, and it was a rough bunch that taught me the fine arts of self-defense. Rough and tough, but with hearts of gold when a fellow needed a friend. Many of them were later to become business leaders of the city.[36]

In spite of friction, the leading weekly newspaper in Stamford (by this time edited by an Irish-born Protestant) was reporting approvingly in 1868 of Father John Fagan's efforts to inculcate temperance, patriotism, and religion in his flock and to form St. Patrick's Roman Catholic Total Abstinence Society. In time, the activities of the newly formed Ancient Order of Hibernians were reported with the same careful respect as the activities of the prestigious Stamford Yacht Club, and the St. Patrick's Day parade was covered with full and sympathetic accounts, indicating "the growing acceptance by the Yankee majority of Irish pride and the growing confidence of the Irish of their role in the community culture."[37]

The Irish increasingly viewed themselves as permanent residents of the town. Although their influence on local policy decisions in town meet-

[34] Feinstein, *Stamford in the Gilded Age,* p. 59.

[35] John Higham, *Strangers in the Land: Patterns of American Nativism: 1860–1925* (New York: Atheneum, 1965), p. 26.

[36] *WPA Federal Writers' Project on the Growth of Bridgeport, Connecticut,* Interview dated March 7, 1940 (Storr's: Ethnic Heritage Project: The Peoples of Connecticut, 1975).

[37] Feinstein, *Stamford in the Gilded Age,* p. 12.

ings was usually limited to voting on issues already formulated by upper-class Yankees in the early years, both Republican and Democratic parties made efforts to cut across class and ethnic lines in their appeals. By 1884, the first Irish residents had begun to be elected to major posts in Stamford, and by 1897—fifty years after the New York-New Haven line brought the first Irish workers to Stamford—an attorney from the Dublin section was elected mayor of the city. Feinstein observes that

> As office holders emerged from the Irish constituency, which remained firmly in the Democratic camp . . . the new leaders closely resembled, in their solid background of professional and entrepreneurial success, the Yankee establishment of both parties.[38]

Stamford, by this time a thriving city of 16,000, had been transformed into a community which had come to terms with its own growth and with the Irish who had contributed so heavily to it.

## THE EFFECT OF DIFFERENT COMMUNITY SOCIAL STRUCTURES

A comparison of the Irish experience in these four cities suggests that tension was virtually unavoidable, given the religious and social differences between the immigrants and the natives. In their favor, the Irish had their determination to work at any job that was available and familiarity with the English language. On the other hand, their sheer numbers presented serious strains for communities that could not, or did not, provide for decent housing or opportunities for workers to move beyond the unskilled level. Philadelphia, with one of the lowest, and Stamford, with one of the highest percentages of Irish newcomers, nevertheless were similar in their provision for both of these needs. In Philadelphia, the Irish building and loan associations made home ownership possible for those who planned to settle there. In Stamford, the majority of the Irish rented in newly constructed blocks of apartments. The Irish were relegated the least desirable sections in both cities and slums clearly emerged, but in neither place did the squalid conditions prevail which marked the early Irish enclaves in Boston and New York. It may be that the Irish who simply disembarked and remained in the latter cities were more destitute—less capable of taking advantage of the opportunities available—whereas in both Philadelphia and Stamford the majority of the Irish had migrated there from other points of debarkation. But more seems to be involved than this.

Philadelphia had a secure feeling about itself and its future. Riots between Protestants and Catholics had occurred in the 1840s, but there is some evidence that Irish Protestant resentment and antipathy figured

[38] *Ibid.*, p. 37.

heavily in the clashes.[39] Given its expansionary view of the future, Philadelphia could afford to include the Irish in it. Previous experience with Irish organizations had been satisfactory, and these same organizations served the new group of immigrants as a focal point for ethnic identity. Politically, the Irish did not capture the city government and were never so completely a one-party minority as in either Boston or New York.

Stamford, on a smaller scale, provided some of the same advantages as Philadelphia. Even though Stamford was as much a Yankee stronghold as Boston, it was enjoying a vigorous and healthy industrial growth made possible by the same railroad line that brought the Irish in. When the conservative Yankee elders finally relinquished their political hold on the town, the Irish who came forward to replace them were not wholly unlike themselves. Whether or not the eminently fair treatment of the Irish in the local weekly newspaper from 1868 on was a major factor in cooling tensions between the two groups can only be a matter for conjecture, but at any rate the Irish were not forced to resort to heavy-handed measures in order to secure a place for themselves in the growing city. In time, the Anglo-Americans simply moved over to make room for them—both physically, by moving to the outskirts of town, and politically, by withdrawing from the contest.

New York, as we have seen, was already politically dominated by the Irish before the famine immigrants arrived. The sheer size and strength of the already existing, though largely Protestant, Irish community gave an entirely different shape to the experience of the famine Irish when they arrived. Furthermore, subsequent waves of less acculturated immigrants from other countries diluted the impact that a single ethnic minority might make on the city. Compared with Boston, New York simply did not have time to waste on brooding antagonism toward any single minority. Thus, it was in Boston, rather than anywhere else, that the Irish fared least well, yet paradoxically it has been the Boston experience that has for many years provided stereotypical images of the Irish in urban America. That Boston is a somewhat unique case has been brought out in recent scholarship. It may be, as Lawrence McCaffrey argues in *The Irish Diaspora in America,* that Boston's Irish of today are *still* different from those who learned how to be Americans in less hostile environments, and that their "intense ghetto identity and paranoia" exemplify the exception rather than the rule in Irish experience.[40]

As this chapter has suggested, not all Irishmen had the same experience, even if they settled in Eastern urban areas, nor did all Americans respond to them in the same way. What the immigrants brought with them

[39] Clark, *The Irish in Philadelphia,* p. 21.

[40] Lawrence J. McCaffrey, *The Irish Diaspora in America* (Bloomington: Indiana University Press, 1976), p. 188.

in background and in hope may have been remarkably homogeneous, but the ways in which they changed as they became Americanized were, at least in part, a product of interaction in the places where they realized their Irish American identities. Nevertheless, the broad outlines of the Irish urban subsociety had taken shape during these early years. It was to be a subsociety marked by conspicuous physical and social boundaries, for the Irish came in too large numbers to go unnoticed and unresented, and they continued their immigration over too long a period to be able later to dismantle their neighborhoods casually. The physical boundaries marked the edges of the first sizable immigrant ghettos to emerge in American cities, the first Kerrytown and Dublin sections of growing industrial towns, and the first transient shanty towns of work gangs formed by the Irish men who moved along the routes of the internal improvement projects for the country's expansion. The social boundaries enclosed the networks of Catholic parishes and schools, the hoodlum gangs, the fire brigades, and the patriotic and self-help organizations, as well as the social evenings in a neighbor's kitchen where the young could meet and the old reminisce, or the gatherings in the neighborhood saloon where men could just relax or pursue their passion for poetry or politics.

In the cities of the Midwest, where the physical and social boundaries of the Irish subsocieties were often more permeable and the reactions on both sides of the boundaries were likely to be less defensive, and in the Far West, where young Irish adventurers who had been attracted by the promise of fast wealth and a new start found the existing society too new to have firmly established boundaries and the Irish too few to establish their own, the conditions that had maintained the Irish subsocieties of the urban East never developed in quite the same way. Those Irish who had ventured westward, to the extent that they found their Irishness a handicap, a discomfort, or simply an irrelevancy, were freer to ignore it and to know that others would do the same. But the vast majority of the Irish had not gone West, and it was the ideas, the institutions, and the activities of those who remained in the urban East that were to predominate.

The Irish had become, in their early years in America, the first large-scale Catholic immigrant wave to interact with the existing Protestant establishment, the first to institutionalize and finance a steady migration of relatives and friends who would permanently join them in America, and the first to make a transition en masse from a folk society to an urban environment. The techniques they developed to protect their religion and their interests in the early years reflected, in part, their cultural heritage from Ireland, for it was there that they had learned to organize for their own defense and to rely on their wits for survival. But their techniques also reflected their capacity to innovate where no past experience could help them, for the big-city political machines were perfected by the Irish in America and the Catholic school system was an Irish innovation. But their techniques also reflected a capacity to borrow ideas from the larger society, for without business skills of their own, they learned how to proceed in business by watching and learning from the Yankees. In this process of assimilation and adaptation, the Irish were creating a subculture that became as distinctively different from the rural culture they had left in Ireland as it was from the ways of the Anglo-Americans. They had become marginal to both ways of life, and had in fact created an Irish American subsociety to shelter this marginality for as long as individual Irish chose to remain within its boundaries.

# CHAPTER FOUR

# *From Shanty to Lace Curtain*

By the early 1900s, the American Irish as a group were in transition from the position of new immigrants, disparagingly called "shanty Irish" by Yankees of the mid-1800s, to a position of middle-class "lace curtain" respectability. Although the transition was marked by increasing numbers of individual successes, as those of longer residence or personal enterprise moved into positions of financial, political, and social prominence, it was largely a group phenomenon—a product of the settling in of the second- and third-generation descendants of the early famine immigrants, who now came to regard themselves, and to be regarded, as acculturated members of an American mosaic.

For the vast majority, the transition was accomplished within social institutions distinct from those of the host society. Just as contacts in Ireland between British Anglicans, Scotch Presbyterians, and Irish Catholics had been structured along lines which prevented significant contact of individual group members at the primary level, so in America there continued to be separate institutional lives, in spite of the acculturation achieved by the early generations. Links with the Anglo-American community were formed through interaction in occupations, and through political activities, but the hostility to Catholicism on the part of the Protestant majority provided a constant reminder to later generations of Irish Americans that social barriers still existed. Many an Irish American went from the cradle to the grave without ever venturing outside the ethnic community, bounded by its familiar network of activities with relatives and friends, served by the parish church, the parochial school, the neighborhood saloon, and the Irish social clubs. That this pattern was eventually broken was partly the result of outside events which decreased the need for, and attractiveness of, the self-enclosed ethnic subsociety.

By the 1880s, waves of newer Catholic immigrants began to arrive in those areas where the Irish were already established. Comparing themselves with the incoming Italians, Poles, and Slovaks, the Irish adjudged themselves not only acculturated but more sophisticated. As Anglo-Americans watched the Irish assert their leadership among the newer immigrants, in politics and in labor unions, even they came to appreciate the mediating role the Irish were playing. Whether providing a model for the newcomers as they struggled to advance a rung on the social ladder, prodding them to learn English so they could participate more easily in labor negotiations, serving as ward-heelers who brought conciliation between opposing ethnic constituencies, or policing the immigrant ghettos of expanding cities, the Irish displayed an extraordinary aptitude for serving as middlemen between the Yankees and the new immigrants.

It was at this point that religious differences came to be regarded as less important than the "racial" similarities, for although the Irish famine immigrants had been defined as racially inferior in the 1840s and 1850s it was only too apparent now in the decades following the 1880s that they had much in common with the Yankees, whatever their religion. Now it was the Catholic immigrants from southern and western Europe who were defined as racially inferior, as well as religiously different, and who, in their efforts to discover what it was to be American, looked to the predominantly Irish Catholic Church, the predominantly Irish political and labor organizations, and the settled Irish neighborhoods for models. In many communities, the Yankee establishment was quite willing to leave to the Irish the task of Americanizing the newest immigrants. By the 1920s, when nativist fears finally led to the enactment of immigrant quotas aimed at stopping the flow of southern and eastern European immigration to the United States, the Irish were increasingly moving into the security of middle-class positions. Their determination to seize the opportunities which had for so long been denied their forebears in Ireland, helped them to advance socio-economically and thus to vacate for the newer waves of immigrants the lower rungs of the social ladder.

Two additional events occurred almost simultaneously to undermine the need for neighborhood and organizational supports which had been necessary to earlier generations of Irish immigrants. One was the disenchantment of many returning World War I veterans with the traditional "shanty" neighborhoods. The second was the successful resolution of the drive to expel the British from Ireland. The establishment of the Irish Free State in 1921 brought to a close the most energetic of the efforts by Irish individuals and organizations to wind up the unfinished business which they were conscious of having left behind them, and permitted them to accept their full Americanization without guilt. The fact that the six northern counties of Ireland remained tied to Britain did not cause undue anguish among the vast majority of Irish Americans, since they had emigrated from the southern and western counties themselves. It was their people, their relatives, their family farms which were finally freed from the ancient domination by England. It was as though—partly, at least, through their efforts—a family responsibility had been fulfilled, and they were now free to attend to any unfinished business in their own affairs.

For those successful Irish Americans who had risen to "lace curtain" respectability in the preceding years, the unfinished business in the 1920s appeared to involve full movement into the mainstream of American social life. It began to appear that the Irish American social organizations which had been established to serve not only the needs of those remaining in ethnic neighborhoods but also the less parochial needs of those who had moved out into professional and upper-class positions were not, after all, quite so necessary. The genuine possibility arose that the old Yankee institutions and clubs would be ready to accept Irish American members, not just as exceptional token Irish, but simply as Americans and social equals. In some communities, particularly in the urban East, this final breakthrough into the mainstream of American social life began only with the disaster of the Depression years, for by this time many Anglo-American clubs and organizations were faced with the dilemma of either accepting Irish members or closing their doors. Yet the readiness of many Irish Americans to merge with the larger society was there by the 1920s. In the remainder of this chapter we will focus on the Irish neighborhood, its institutional life, and the links it maintained with Anglo society through occupational and political activities, each of which underwent change as part of this transition.

## THE IRISH AMERICAN NEIGHBORHOOD

As we have already seen, the physical properties of ethnic neighborhoods varied according to the host communities in which they developed, but the social qualities were less varied. Within the neighborhood there was warmth, sociability, and belonging, whether it was in a crowded urban slum or in the Dublin section of a small town. As in Ireland, so in America—the ties of family and friendship were the basis of all other activities. What might look like a shanty to the Yankee was home for the Irish family. What might look like a slum from the outside was a familiar haven for the Irish child growing up in the latter half of the nineteenth century and into the twentieth. What might look like an effort to attain gentility *was* gentility to the Irish family.

The constant replenishment of the Irish community by immigrants being "brought out" from Ireland to join the American side of the family kept interest in Irish affairs strong, permitted close ties with the old ways, and sustained much of the ethnic consciousness felt by the first generation. Between 1861 and 1910, well over 300,000 in each decade continued to leave Irish ports for the United States. After 1910, the numbers declined, but still, by 1970, close to five million Irish immigrants had entered the United States from Irish ports alone since 1820 (see Table 2). The vast majority found relatives waiting in America to greet them. If the new arrivals brought welcome news from the old country, they also permitted the American Irish to sense clearly how much progress they had made in the new country. The welcoming relatives could display their Americanization for sisters, cousins, and nephews just "brought out"—and the newcomers were impressed.

*TABLE 2*

*THE IRISH AND OTHER IMMIGRANT GROUPS TO AMERICA*

| Decade | Irish | All Immigrants |
|---|---|---|
| 1820–1830 | 54,338 | 151,824 |
| 1831–1840 | 207,381 | 599,125 |
| 1841–1850 | 780,719 | 1,713,251 |
| 1851–1860 | 914,119 | 2,598,214 |
| 1861–1870 | 435,778 | 2,314,824 |
| 1871–1880 | 436,871 | 2,812,191 |
| 1881–1890 | 655,482 | 5,246,613 |
| 1891–1900 | 390,179 | 3,687,564 |
| 1901–1910 | 339,065 | 8,795,386 |
| 1911–1920 | 146,181 | 5,735,811 |
| 1921–1930 | 220,591 | 4,107,209 |
| 1931–1940 | 13,167 | 528,431 |
| 1941–1950 | 25,377 | 1,035,039 |
| 1951–1960 | 57,332 | 2,515,479 |
| 1961–1970 | 37,461 | 3,321,777 |
| *TOTAL FOR THE 150-YEAR PERIOD* | 4,713,868 | 45,162,638 |

*Note:* The data for the Irish include only those who came to the United States from Ireland and not those who emigrated from other countries. Between 1820 and 1850, the Irish comprised 42.3 percent of all American immigrants. They were 35.2 percent of those between 1851 and 1860. In the 1961–1970 decade, the Irish were only 1.1 percent of all immigrants. Overall, they represent 10.4 percent. Statistics are based on U.S. Immigration and Naturalization Service *Annual Reports.*

Source: Frank A. Stone, *The Irish of Connecticut* (Storrs: Ethnic Heritage Studies Series: The Peoples of Connecticut, 1975), Unit 3, p. 22.

The neighborhoods to which the immigrants came were likely to be predominantly Irish in the early years. For those who had settled in old established communities along the eastern seaboard, the feeling of being unwelcome in the Yankee districts—or of being more welcome and secure in the Irish—helped to maintain Irish American enclaves well into the twentieth century. But no matter how large the city, or where it was located, the self-contained neighborhood had the feeling of a small town or village and was part of what Mike Royko, describing the ethnic neighborhoods of Chicago as they existed in the early years of this century, called a larger "ethnic state."[1]

In the Irish South Side of Chicago, the neighborhood-town of Bridgeport was "a community that drank out of the beer pail and ate out of the lunch bucket . . . a union neighborhood. They bought small frame homes or rented flats. It had as many Catholic schools as public schools, and the

[1] Mike Royko, *Boss: Richard J. Daley of Chicago* (New York: New American Library, 1971), p. 30.

enrollment at the parochial schools was bigger." The South Side Irish neighborhood was part of the larger ethnic state of Ireland, surrounded by Germany to the north, Poland to the northwest, Italy and Israel to the west, and Bohemia and Lithuania to the southwest. And even with your eyes closed, Royko points out, you could tell which state you were in "by the odors of the food stores and the open kitchen windows, the sound of the foreign or familiar language, and by whether a stranger hit you in the head with a rock." He continues:

> But in the neighborhood, you were safe. At least if you did not cross beyond, say, to the other side of the school. While it might be part of your ethnic state, it was still the edge of another neighborhood, and their gang was just as mean as your gang. So, for a variety of reasons, ranging from convenience to fear to economics, people stayed in their own neighborhood, loving it, enjoying the closeness, the friendliness, the familiarity, and trying to save enough money to move out.[2]

Yet by the 1930s, children whose parents had settled earlier in such communities were increasingly entering high school and beginning to wonder whether they were perhaps missing something. A third-generation young Irish American from a lower-middle-class family in one of the Irish neighborhoods of a Connecticut city described his discontent when he was interviewed in 1939, at the age of 21:

> We lived in a typical two-family house with a small garden and lawn. Our furniture was bought at the local department stores—sets of veneered wood, lace curtains, sentimental pictures, and lots of photographs, plants, and ferns. As a child I played with the neighborhood children. At the parochial school my classmates were Irish, Italian, Negro, and Slovak. I played with them, but only at school. In high school, I found my first knowledge of life and interests dissimilar to my surroundings. It was there I discovered that there was a more interesting and fuller life than that of myself and my friends. I tried to become a part of it, but found it difficult because of lack of money, background, and the snobbishness of my more fortunate classmates. As a result, I read a great deal—the books available in the public library—and spent the rest of my time with fellows of my own kind.[3]

An elderly third-generation Irish American interviewed in 1975 describes the slow abandonment of the neighborhood in New Britain, Connecticut, where he had grown up as a child, and where he later returned to spend his retirement among the few who remained of those he had known:

> This territory of Dublin Hill was, I would say, 95 percent Irish a hundred years ago. Either they came over from the old country, or their parents or grandparents had. The factories were beginning to boom. New Britain

[2] *Ibid.*, pp. 31–33.

[3] Interview with "Patrick Doe," *WPA Federal Writers' Project on the Growth of Bridgeport, Connecticut* (Storrs: Ethnic Heritage Project: The Peoples of Connecticut, 1975).

> doubled its population from 5,000 to 10,000 in ten years, and from 10,000 to 20,000 in the next ten years. You see, this town was originally settled by people from England—Yankees, we called them, but in those days there was Dublin Hill that was an Irish settlement, and then there was a place named after a freed slave—Nigger Hill—that was Irish too. I guess the Irish started coming to Dublin Hill around 1840. My grandmother died here in 1853—that's her monument up in the cemetery around Dublin Hill. There's still a few of the old-timers left, or their descendants, but the majority are dead and buried. Now Dublin Hill is Italian, Slavic, very few Irish, very few. Right after World War I they started leaving. It's like this: my brother was born and brought up here, but after he came out of the service he got married, and he and his wife wouldn't live here. They say this district isn't good enough for them, so they've gone to a district where I used to shoot rabbits. These people whose parents owned their own homes on Dublin Hill—when they died their children sold the homes and went to outlying places that were farmland. It's the flight to suburbia.[4]

Some individual families of the second and third generation had started to leave the Irish neighborhoods well before 1900, but mass movement did not begin until later because, although a few had achieved conspicious financial and social success by the turn of the century, and a sizable middle-class minority had emerged, the majority were still struggling members of the working class. For them, it was still more comfortable to live in neighborhoods with the feeling of "a little county in Ireland," even though they were committed to a future in America.

## ORGANIZATIONAL LIFE

Cut off from the traditional sociability of the rural hamlet in Ireland, set apart from the Yankee community by stereotyped reactions and anti-Catholic sentiment, the first immigrants had contrived to create their own complex network of social life which was quite different from, but substituted for, that of the old country. The need for ethnic identity, for recreation, for mutual aid, for the performance of religious obligations, and for support of political interests in Ireland and in America provided themes around which Irish organizations formed. Within the organizations, self-esteem could be achieved, social competition entered into, and avenues for advancement explored in ways that helped the Irish adapt as individuals and as a group to the larger society.

### The Neighborhood Saloon

At the least formal level, the neighborhood saloons—the "poor man's clubs"—with their male clientele crossing all social levels, continued the familiar institution of the public house in Ireland. Wittke comments that

[4] Interview with Mr. B, *Oral History Project* (Storrs: Ethnic Heritage Project: The Peoples of Connecticut, 1975).

> Many of the Irishman's troubles and much of his unfavorable reputation were directly traceable to too great a devotion to the bottle. . . . Perhaps it was Irish love of sociability that led so many to become saloon keepers and bartenders. The percentage of Irish liquor dealers was high; the business required relatively little capital; customers were plentiful; and the saloon, in the early days, was an entree to politics.[5]

Here in the saloon were camaraderie and consolation for the worker, a forum for social and political discourse for the concerned and the calculating, and a club-like atmosphere for those who were unlikely to join more formal organizations. The saloon keeper was a familiar and respected figure, providing guidance, credit, and political contacts.

A first-generation Irish woman describes her position as a saloon keeper's wife in Bridgeport, Connecticut, during the early years of this century:

> I've always lived around this neighborhood. It's where my sister settled, and therefore a second home to me. I was married here in Saint Mary's Church, and had a large wedding as my husband had a very prosperous tavern—at that time called a saloon. He was able to have a couple of bartenders, and we were considered very well off—in fact, so much so that at times I had two maids in my home. In the days of the saloon, many political questions were settled for the district over the bar. Just before election day, both parties came around treating the house. Drinks were all on the party leaders. Tonight it might be the Republicans, tomorrow night the Democrats. It wasn't just your district; it was leaders from every district in the city.[6]

Though the owners and patrons of the Irish neighborhood saloons were viewed with distaste by Yankees who felt they routinely violated Puritan standards, for the Irish the sporadic threats that the saloons would be closed by municipal regulations—as well as the larger threat of nationwide prohibition on the sale of alcohol—represented more than just the possible loss of a friendly drink at the bar. As the saloon keeper's wife indicated, "many political questions were settled for the district over the bar." The eventual success of the Anti-Saloon League's national campaign to prohibit the manufacture and sale of alcohol throughout the country thoroughly disrupted the web of social and political activity that had centered in and around the neighborhood saloons. With the Prohibition Amendment in 1917, the institution of the public house came to a legal, if temporary, end. For many among the Irish, it all seemed quite senseless.

### Total Abstinence Societies

Although the Anti-Saloon League had been primarily a rural Protestant phenomenon, there were those in the Irish community, especially among the women, who also viewed excesses in drinking with real concern. Aware

[5] Carl Wittke, *The Irish in America,* (New York: Russell and Russell, 1970), p. 48.
[6] Interview with Mrs. O (1939), *WPA Federal Writers' Project.*

that drink, "the curse of the Irish," was part of the negative stereotype that had been earned in America, but also anxious to curb the ever-present threat of alcoholism, the Catholic Total Abstinence Union had been formed as a national organization in 1866 with headquarters in Philadelphia. In all the major cities, priests encouraged the formation of local chapters and labored to counteract the appeal of the neighborhood saloon. Although these associations were closely related in their activities to the Christian Temperance Union, they remained socially separate from their Anglo counterpart. In special halls built to provide sociability and support for non-drinkers, they offered social bonds and recreation for those willing to "take the pledge." For many young men who had viewed the havoc created in their own homes, and in those of friends, because of drinking excesses, they made good sense.

An Irish American resident of New Britain, Connecticut, describes his reasons for having joined such a club in his youth:

> I took a pledge not to drink. Our club's name was the Young Men's Temperance and Benevolent Society. I'll tell you, I saw too many Irish families getting ruined by liquor. You know the Irish are heavy drinkers. I said to my mother, "Ma, the saloon people will never get rich on me, because how can a woman have any love for a man who comes home drunk, and beats her up, and breaks her furniture, and the kids are in rags? If I was a woman, I wouldn't stand for that from any man." And up to the time she died, my mother said, "You are a wanderer, but I don't worry about you because you don't drink."[7]

Although the total abstinence societies provided a respectable male alternative to the sociability of the saloon, the traditional cultural supports for drinking remained strong among working-class men. In the early years, liquor was often provided as part of the wages in laboring jobs, and hard drinking in the company of other men became part of the bachelor group life style that had developed both in Ireland and America from the 1840s onward. Those who rose socially—sometimes with the earnings of successful breweries—did not join the common men's chapter of the local abstinence society, but they too were conscious of the need to counteract the negative stereotype of the drunken Irishman, and were often conspicuous in their abstention. The total abstinence societies are no longer functioning organizations, but the priests who hear confessions are still issuing the warning they contained. One Irish American educator, recalling his college years, still remembers the priest who responded to his confession of too many beers the night before with the words, "You must take care, my son. Drinking is a problem we Irish have."[8]

[7] Interview with Mr. B, *Oral History Project.*
[8] Marjorie Fallows, private collection (1976).

## Fraternal Organizations

In the early years of loneliness and perplexity in America, fraternal organizations were formed to share the financial burdens, to provide aid for new arrivals, and to celebrate the bonds of Irish identity. The Charitable Irish Society in Boston and the Friendly Sons of St. Patrick in New York had been established in the 1700s, and were already venerable organizations with a Protestant Irish cast by the 1800s. There followed the Ancient Order of Hibernians, founded in 1836 in New York by a charter from Ireland permitting American Catholics of Irish extraction to become members of this fraternal and insurance society. Other organizations, like the Knights of Columbus, began as local parish groups whose aim was to provide self-help and social benefits for the Irish communicants. In the years after the initial founding of the Knights of Columbus in the rectory of Saint Mary's Church in New Haven, in 1881, priests who accompanied the workers on internal improvement projects in the developing lands to the west found it a suitable organization to bring their men together, and so it spread through the towns along the routes the Irish construction workers had taken. Although started by Irishmen, the Knights of Columbus had never been specifically limited to the Irish and gradually came to include Catholics of other ethnic backgrounds.

By the early 1900s the need for fraternal organizations was less intense. An Irish American, describing the dying out of interest in Irish organizations apparent already in the 1930s in Bridgeport, Connecticut, noted:

> At the turn of the century, most of the Irish families were very active as far as society goes. There were many Irish organizations—the Ancient Order of Hibernians, the Hibernian Rifles, and many other nationalistic clubs flourished. Within the past few decades the Irish have lost their racial identity, and their interest in nationalistic clubs has waned until it no longer exists. Today the third and fourth generations have already lost their desire to be called "Irish." The only time you get Irish groups together that include first generation as well as later generations is at the religious services and church socials.[9]

Yet, as sometimes happens, the socially mobile later generations of Irish Americans, who had successfully proved to themselves that they no longer needed to band together for mutual self-help and sociability, eventually started to show sparks of interest in the culture they had lost. Two Irish American newspaper editors—Thomas Murray of *The Daily Sun* in Lawrence, Massachusetts, and John Boyle O'Reilly of *The Boston Pilot*—had already foreseen in 1897 that the time would come when later generations would have enough detachment from the miseries of the early years to display a real interest in the circumstances of the Irish immigration to America. Viewed as history or as cultural appreciation, the reacquaintance

[9] John Driscoll, Background Paper on the Irish in Bridgeport, Connecticut (1939), *WPA Federal Writers' Project.*

with their Irish heritage began to seem a worthwhile—perhaps a necessary—goal for at least some in the Irish American community. But the activities of more recently founded Irish American organizations, like the Irish Home Society described in Chapter 6 by one of its early members, bore little relationship to the sterner needs of those who had formed fraternal organizations in the 1700s and 1800s to share memories of the past and provide solace and protection in the present.

### Irish Nationalist Groups

Because the Irish community was constantly replenished from Ireland, and because of easy access to Irish news through the Irish American press, organizational activity frequently centered around ideological, monetary, and military efforts to aid Ireland. Although the majority of the rural immigrants had identified more with the town or county from which they came, the effect of contact in America with countrymen from other parts of Ireland served to broaden their concern and to focus attention on Irish nationalism.[10] The leaders of the Irish nationalist movement were the more idealistic and educated members of the Irish American community who were determined to free Ireland and to remodel it in the image of America. William Shannon presents the thesis that this "transference of values was an understandable, natural way for millions of uprooted people to assimilate themselves to a new country—that is, by transposing the strange values of their new country back to the familiar setting of the old country."[11] In so doing, he suggests, they were educating themselves as Americans, whether or not they were immediately successful in freeing Ireland.

The nationalist efforts to bring pressure to bear on Britain, and to win concessions—or better yet, freedom—for Ireland, ranged from simple fund raising to the mounting of military invasions. As early as the 1860s, concern for the revolutionary cause in Ireland had led various Irish Emigrant Aid societies to broaden their scope to include promoting Irish independence. About the same time, the Fenian Brotherhood was organized in New York as a political and para-military organization, similar to those being simultaneously organized in England and Ireland, dedicated to active intervention in the cause of a free Ireland. During the Civil War, Fenian organizers freely recruited their own military organization from within the Union Army, and in 1863 men were even given leave from their army obligations to attend the first Fenian Convention in Chicago. In 1865 alone, $228,000 was raised by the Fenian Brotherhood in America, and in the following year the Fenian forces—known as the Irish Republican Brotherhood—launched an ill-starred attempt to invade Canada in the belief that Britain's hand could be forced by holding Canada hostage. Even though the Fenians met with some military success in Canada, the American govern-

[10] For an excellent discussion of Irish-American nationalism, see Thomas N. Brown, *Irish-American Nationalism:1870–1890* (New York: J. B. Lippincott Co., 1966).

[11] William Shannon, *The American Irish* (New York: Macmillan, 1963), p. 113.

ment forced a withdrawal to avoid possible British reprisals. In the following year, a Fenian revolt in Ireland also failed. Many Irish had been involved in the movement, if not directly then through their emotional and monetary support. After the failure of direct intervention and increasingly clear indications that the United States government would no longer permit open Fenian revolutionary activities, a more disciplined secret society—the Clan na Gael—was started as an alternative organization, and by the 1870s was beginning to absorb the divided and demoralized Fenian movement.

While these and other less activist organizations did not directly involve the majority of Irish Americans, who were concerned with the more immediate problems of making their own way in America, the activities of those who were in the nationalist movement were often viewed with sympathy. In his book on Irish American nationalism, Thomas N. Brown has argued that many middle-class Irish Americans who were leaders in nationalist organizations such as the Fenian Brotherhood and the Clan were actually less concerned with vengeance against either Britain or American nativists than with promoting social respectability for the Irish in America by freeing their homeland and themselves from the stigma of bondage.[12] Thus, the activities of these organizations served a dual purpose: as emotional rallying points for those in search of identity and respectability and as an institution through which they could exert political pressure to free their homeland.

For its part, the American government was embarrassed and provoked, but at the same time influenced, by the constant pressure from Irish American nationalists. The British lamented that in times of previous Irish unrest they had been able to contain and subdue the revolutionaries. Now, on the other hand, a second Irish nation existed in America. There was little they could do about it, for it was equally hostile, politically powerful, willing to provide money, and totally out of reach. The Irish had discovered that the power which they had failed to achieve in their homeland could now be wielded in its defense from across the Atlantic. Even though it would be years before the Irish Free State would be created in 1921, the emotional involvement of thousands of Irish Americans in the nationalist effort provided a source of ethnic identity and cohesiveness. The goals of the nationalist movement, if not necessarily its methods, were close to the hearts of men and women who remembered that they had virtually been forced out of their homeland.

## LINKS WITH THE LARGER SOCIETY

While the nationalist movement created bonds within the American Irish community and maintained close bonds with Ireland itself, it did not provide links with the social world of non-Catholic, non-Irish Americans.

[12] Brown, *Irish-American Nationalism*, pp. 38-41.

As we have seen, the institutional life of the neighborhood, the Catholic fraternal organizations, and the nationalist movement all reinforced some degree of separateness from the larger community. At the same time, the structural pluralism which determined that the American Irish would maintain their own ethnic network of relationships, apart from the social life of the wider society, did not necessarily prevent their forming links with those of different backgrounds in their jobs. Insofar as the work was entirely with, or for, others of the same ethnic identity, the contact could be a weak one; but as leadership emerged in the Irish community among successful businessmen, professionals, and labor and political leaders, links with the larger community had to be forged.

The conditions which led to rising Irish discontent with the position of the ordinary working man in industry, and which brought the Irish into prominence in labor union activity, are illustrated by H. M. Gitelman's study of Waltham, Massachusetts, for the period of 1850 to 1890.[13] Like other expanding industrial towns along the eastern seaboard, Waltham drew on Irish immigrants for its unskilled work force. Gitelman's study concerns itself with the extent of discrimination against the Irish after they were already in the work force, rather than with the discrimination which initially brought out the "No Irish Need Apply" notices in the early years. In Waltham, between 1850 and 1890, the majority of men in the arduous and unstable day laboring jobs were Irish-born—both earlier immigrants and more recent arrivals. The American-born sons were increasingly avoiding day labor and moving into higher status work in retail trade and services as self-employed entrepreneurs. By 1880, stable keeping, furniture moving, and contracting had become predominantly Irish fields, and a limited number of professional men had emerged. Yet self-employment was a hazardous route because the investment of capital and the rate of failure were high. Less than half of the self-employment ventures between 1880 and 1890 survived the ten-year period.

For those Irish-born men with too little capital and skill to start in business for themselves, the mills and factories provided the only opportunities for jobs. Here a vicious cycle developed, for it was virtually impossible to move from unskilled to skilled or supervisory jobs in the major industries. Even after years of continuous service, the Irish were seldom promoted to supervisory positions because the companies went outside to hire Yankee supervisors. Given the low wages of the unskilled workers, the sons of the laboring fathers were forced to enter similarly unskilled jobs to help out at home. The combination of early entry into the labor market plus lack of advancement meant that a man or boy in the last half of the 1800s had three options: (1) remaining permanently in an unskilled position in a Yankee-run industry, with little possibility of learning the skills needed for advancement, (2) entering one of the Irish-dominated fields like

[13] H. M. Gitelman, "No Irish Need Apply: Patterns of and Response to Ethnic Discrimination in the Labor Market," *Labor History,* 14 (Winter 1973), 56–68.

contracting, which involved work and interaction with other Irish, or (3) taking a gamble on self-employment.

It is small wonder that the Irish, with their concern for the uses of power, and their political awareness, should increasingly have been attracted to labor unions as a way of protecting their interests in the industrial areas where they were occupationally trapped as they were in Waltham. Working-class discontent erupted in the 1880s, with tens of thousands of workers going out on strike across the country. The union organizers and leaders who emerged from this awakening of the working man were drawn heavily from Irish ranks. This was the situation when the still newer waves of unskilled immigrants from southern and eastern Europe arrived on the scene at the end of the nineteenth century. Not only were the Irish in positions of union strength, but they were increasingly the straw-bosses with experience and skill on the job. They had emerged as the mediators between the new arrivals and the larger middle-class Anglo-American society. For the new immigrants, they seemed the prototype of the "real American," and they accepted the designation as appropriate.

By the turn of the century, strikes in the Chicago meat-packing industry spurred a government investigation into the relationship between union activity and immigrant assimilation. Reported in a 1905 Bulletin of the Bureau of Labor, the investigation concluded that the unions helped, rather than hindered, immigrant adjustment to American life, and included an appreciative comment on the role of the Irish, and to a lesser extent of the Germans, in bringing this about:

> The unions in the stock yards are controlled by the Irish, ably assisted by the Germans. . . . It is here that the practical utility of learning English is first brought home forcibly to the immigrants. In all other of his associations not only does his own language suffice, but, for reasons that can be well understood, shrewd leaders minimize the importance of learning any other. . . . In his trade union the Slav mixes with the Lithuanian, the German, and the Irish, and this is the only place they do mix until, by virtue of this intercourse and this mixing, clannishness is to a degree destroyed, and a social mixing along other lines comes naturally into play. . . . It is true that this Americanizing is being done by the Irish and the Germans, but it is Americanizing nevertheless, and is being done as rapidly as the material to work on will permit, and very well indeed. . . . The Union begins by teaching the immigrant that his wages are not so good as another man's . . . but the union gets him to compare himself not with what he was in Lithuania, but with some German or Irish family.[14]

Relations between the Irish and other immigrants were by no means always amicable. At the close of the Civil War for example, Irish, German, and Welsh Pennsylvania coal miners complained of newer immigrants who

[14] Bulletin of the Bureau of Labor, No. 56 (January 1905), pp. 4–8, as reported in Stanley Feldstein and Lawrence Costello, *The Ordeal of Assimilation: A Documentary History of the White Working Class: 1830s to the 1970s* (Garden City: Anchor Books, 1974), pp. 344–348.

were endangering their jobs, and in the 1870s riots erupted between the striking Irish and the Polish, Italian, and French Canadian strikebreakers who were brought in to replace them.[15] Nonetheless, Protestant Americans had, to some extent, already delegated to the Irish the mediator's job of dealing with the new waves of Catholic immigrants—as union leader, ward-heeler, or local policeman. The Irish had not, by the turn of the century, become fully acceptable to the Yankee world themselves, but they were close enough to being part of the larger society so they could serve as acceptable substitutes for it, and links with it, where the newer immigrants were concerned. Their grasp of what was needed to bring order out of the potential chaos of conflicting interests in ethnically mixed occupational groups and political districts led, almost inevitably, to their assumption of leadership.

The position of the Irish as mediators was not necessarily a disinterested one. In their assumption of leadership roles in unions and in politics, they were choosing careers that required a minimum of education yet provided upward mobility for working-class people. As Shannon observes:

> Politics was their career. Like every other profession, it was expected to reward its practitioners with money, prestige and, if possible, security. It was generally expected that a politician would make money out of his office, collaterally if not directly, and that if he lost he would be "taken care of" in a sinecure. . . . Because the public payroll was the politician's only resource, he was expected to use it to succor his family and dependents.[16]

Nevertheless, the Irish knew how to conciliate the various ethnic groups in the political wards where they vied for election and in the labor unions where they aspired to high office. In the process of fulfilling their role as mediators, the Irish acquired status and power in their own community as well as in the eyes of the larger society, which now included new immigrants whose differences from the Anglo world were so conspicuous as to make the Irish seem highly Americanized.

That the Irish compared themselves favorably with the Italians, Jews, Slovaks, and others who made up this new wave of foreigners is not hard to believe. A second-generation Irish American woman, now in her eighties, remembers her amazement and disdain at first coming into contact with newly arrived immigrants in the Massachusetts village where she grew up: "When the Italians first moved here to work in the woolen mill, we used to go down to watch them washing their clothes in the river. They really were different from us. It seemed so—well, odd—to see them doing that."[17] Conversely, the newer immigrants equated the Irish with the larger American society, if one can judge from the candid admission of a Czechoslovakian woman recalling her girlhood in Stamford, Connecticut:

[15] Wittke, *The Irish in America,* p. 225.
[16] Shannon, *The American Irish,* p. 65.
[17] Fallows, private collection.

I used to wish I had an American name like the kids in our school who were Kellys and O'Briens and Sullivans. I had one of those foreign names nobody could pronounce. But when I married I got over the problem. I'm a Kelly now.[18]

But links with the larger society were also forged in areas other than those of unions and politics; in many cities the insecurity of the job market made civil service occupations seem particularly attractive. An Irish mother might hope her son would become a priest or a lawyer, but she might be quite content if he became a policeman or fireman, or worked for the post office. In communities like Boston, which had limited occupational opportunities for the Irish, he was quite likely to do so. By the early twentieth century the Irish were no longer outsiders to American life. Although their ranks were perpetually reinforced by the arrival of new immigrants, this group was no longer of overwhelming proportions, and the receiving community was well able to help them establish themselves quickly. Second and third generations of Irish American children were increasingly attending high school, and the more affluent were sending their youngsters to Catholic preparatory schools and on to colleges. Occupationally, the Irish were moving into a wider range of fields than any other ethnic minority and were represented in banking, insurance, industry, the professions, entertainment, publishing, the stock market, and both elective and appointive political posts. The new wave of immigrants had displaced the Irish as the current concern, and at least that part of Ireland with which the famine immigrants had most closely identified was free of Britain. On the eve of the Depression, it may have seemed that the worst was over, and that the deprivations of the past had been forgotten.

[18] *Ibid.*

C H A P T E R F I V E

# Status and Social Mobility

In the 1930s and 1940s, when sociologists first began to pay serious attention to the analysis and measurement of social status differences in American communities, the position of the Irish received relatively little attention. Already the best established of the immigrant groups in ethnically mixed communities, the majority of the Irish had moved into the working class and lower-middle class, and a small but recognizable group of businessmen and professionals had emerged at the upper-middle- and even the upper-class levels. Research conducted by W. Lloyd Warner and his colleagues in Newburyport, Massachusetts, during the 1930s showed that the social class distribution for the Irish as a group included 13 percent in the lower-lower class, 54 percent in the working class (Warner's "upper-lower"), 28 percent in the lower-middle, and 6 percent in the upper-middle. When the third generation of native-born Irish was considered separately, however, only 2 percent remained in the lower-lower class, 39 percent were in the working class, 42 percent were now lower-middle, and 17 percent were in the upper-middle.[1] Clearly, each successive generation, even in this conservative New England community, included a larger proportion in the upper reaches of the stratification order.

The sociological thinking of the time, based largely on the Newburyport research, tended to assume that once a substantial number in any nonracial ethnic group had reached the stage of assimilation represented by the Irish, the group would gradually dissolve its ethnic neighborhoods and social organizations and, after a period of marginality, simply be absorbed into the dominant group as class interests began to take precedence over ethnic interests. How long the period of marginality might be, or what it might entail, was not clearly forecast, nor was it clear whether this would be an experience of the pioneering few who reached the upper social levels ahead of the rest, or a phenomenon involving the entire group. The Irish were, in fact, the first large immigrant group to test the proposition that ethnic identity would no longer be of major significance to those who were entering their second, third, and fourth generations in this country, and who had, as a group, entered the middle status levels. We have already seen that the marginality represented by what Milton Barron in 1949 referred to as the "intermediate ethnic sta-

[1] W. Lloyd Warner and Leo Srole, *The Social Systems of American Ethnic Groups* (New Haven: Yale University Press, 1945), pp. 71–2.

tus" of the Irish[2] had proved useful in mediating between the newer immigrants and the established Americans. But it was also true that marginality carried with it a subjective burden of anxiety about where one fitted in. Thus, if the Irish of the 1930s and 1940s were of relatively little concern to the students of social status, social status was, nevertheless, of major concern to the Irish.

By the 1930s, Alfred Smith—the first Catholic of Irish origin to be nominated by a major party for the presidency—had just been defeated after a campaign which renewed old social and religious antagonisms. Young Irish American writers like Eugene O'Neill, F. Scott Fitzgerald, John O'Hara, and James Farrell were winning national attention with literary works which captured the uncertainties of those who found their goals just out of reach. The Great Depression brought reminders, for those who had recently won middle-class status, that security was a fragile thing. Even the more affluent, who were leaving ethnic neighborhoods for the suburbs, discovered that wealth did not necessarily buy acceptance in the more prestigious social clubs of Yankee "society." In short, many second-, third-, and fourth-generation American Irish had become conscious that, although they had won a new measure of political and economic power, there were still difficulties involved in converting these gains into security, acceptance, and prestige.

Though the Irish had come to America with deeply ingrained awareness of class distinctions, the mere consciousness of such distinctions seldom eliminates the desire to transcend them when social mobility emerges as a real possibility. In fact, a recurring theme, when American Irish talk about themselves, has been their social ambition and their preoccupation with success. For the fortunate few, the winning of political power, the amassing of fortunes, and the emergence of an Irish "society" have conspicuously demonstrated this ambition and subsequent success, but the position of the more typical descendants of the Irish immigrants has, until very recently, received little attention.

In the opening paragraph of this book, the Irish Americans were described as very nearly a "lost statistical category." If we want to capture the socioeconomic progress and life style of a group, however, we need reliable statistical evidence of what it has been doing. It would help to know, for instance, just how many Americans are of Irish origin, how many generations they have been in this country, where they live, and whether they are Catholic or Protestant. To discuss socioeconomic status and mobility, we need information about occupations, incomes, and educational levels, and some basis for comparing these with the levels achieved by former generations. Such information is available for a variety of other ethnic groups, but can still only laboriously be pieced together for the Irish.

The profile that is just now emerging from recent studies contains

[2] Milton Barron, "Intermediacy: Conceptualization of Irish Status in America," *Social Forces,* 27 (March 1949), 256–63.

some surprises about Irish Americans, and demonstrates that unchallenged assumptions have led to erroneous conclusions about the accomplishments of Irish Catholics, simply because a few key statistical facts were missing from the analysis. In its most simplistic form, the interplay between unchallenged assumptions and erroneous conclusions can be illustrated by the following sequence of statements:

1. Irish Americans are Catholics.

2. Catholics in America have lower levels of achievement than Protestants.

3. Irish Americans, therefore, have fallen short of substantial success because of their beliefs and behavior as Catholics.

The scientific detective work that has uncovered the fallacies in this reasoning is worth tracing, if only as an object lesson in the danger of unexamined assumptions and as a warning about the hazards of applying general conclusions to specific cases. Needless to say, all of the assumptions contain falsehoods.

## IRISH AMERICAN ACHIEVEMENT AND NATIONAL ORIGIN

When the United States Census departed from its usual practice of identifying only first- and second-generation immigrants (by country of origin and nativity of father) to include a question on ethnic origin as part of its November 1969 Current Population Survey, its 1971 Current Population Report on that survey provided the first comprehensive description of Irish Americans as a national origin group. In the Census report, nearly 7 percent—13,282,000—claim Ireland as their ancestral home.[3] Since the question was not intended as an indication of religious affiliation (the Census cannot and does not ask a religious question), the data merely describe the self-identified decendants of any Irish who may have immigrated at any period.

But we recall from previous discussion that Irish immigration to the United States occurred in three distinct, but overlapping, waves: (1) the largely Protestant (Scotch-Irish) immigrants of the Colonial period who tended to settle south and west of Pennsylvania; (2) the Catholic famine immigrants of the mid-nineteenth century who tended to settle in the middle Atlantic and New England states; and (3) the steady but dwindling stream of largely Catholic immigrants who "came out" in subsequent decades. Because immigration statistics were unrecorded before 1820, and were of questionable accuracy even during the famine era, there has been

[3] United States Bureau of the Census, *Current Population Report,* Series P-20, No. 221; "Characteristics of the Population by Ethnic Origin: November 1969" (Washington, D.C.: U.S. Government Printing Office, 1971), p.4.

no reliable way of estimating the numbers of early immigrants whose descendants might still identify as Irish in origin. The Census profile of Irish Americans as a national origin group, therefore, would contain an unspecified number of the descendants of the earlier Protestant Irish in addition to the more recent, and largely Catholic, immigrants.

The picture that emerges from the data contained in the 1971 Current Population Report indicates that, as a national origin group, Irish Americans match or slightly exceed the national average on such measures as education, income, and occupation. They appear to have joined the American mainstream at the midpoint of accomplishment. In the 25 to 34 age group, the median number of school years completed was 12.6, compared with the national median of 12.2, whereas for the 35 and over age group it was identical with the national median of 12.0.[4] In terms of 1969 family income, the Irish median income was $8,127—slightly above the national median of $7,894.[5] The employment status of Irish males over 16 showed 29.6 percent in high-level white collar jobs (managerial and professional) compared with 28.2 percent nationally.[6] For women, 20.7 percent were in these kinds of jobs, compared with 18.7 percent nationally.[7] In short, the Census profile suggests a steady, if not spectacular, progress toward a position of acceptance and success in America.

## IRISH AMERICAN ACHIEVEMENT AND RELIGIOUS AFFILIATION

Since neither religious affiliation nor time of ancestral immigration was available for the national origin group identified by the Census, it was impossible to determine whether Catholicism had played a major part—through its teachings and practices, or through the discrimination it engendered—in accounting for the Irish accomplishments. It has, after all, always been the religious component rather than the national origin component of ethnicity that tended to define the Irish experience. On this subject the Census was mute, but Harold Abramson provided a clue to Irish religious affilation in 1973 when he reported on a National Opinion Research Center (NORC) survey of over 2,000 Catholic Americans originally interviewed in 1964.[8] His analysis of the survey data in *Ethnic Diversity in Catholic America* led to an estimate of 8,300,000 Catholic Irish in America[9]—a surprising five million fewer than the 13,282,000 in the na-

[4] *Ibid.*, p.19.
[5] *Ibid.*, p. 22.
[6] *Ibid.*, p. 23.
[7] *Ibid.*, p. 24.
[8] Harold Abramson, *Ethnic Diversity in Catholic America* (New York: John Wiley and Sons, 1973).
[9] *Ibid.*, p. 19.

tional origin group identified by the Census. Was the discrepancy due to sampling error, or were close to 40 percent of the American Irish in the Census survey really Protestant? Subsequent studies have shown that the latter explanation is the correct one, and that the actual percent may even be closer to 50.[10]

Such a large proportion of Irish Protestants not only runs counter to the assumption that to be Irish is to be Catholic, but it raises further questions about who the Protestant Irish are. Because they are disproportionately rural and southern, the best estimate is that 80 to 90 percent are descendants of the Ulster migration of the 1700s or of emigrants from southern Ireland who had converted to Protestantism during Penal times and, like the Scotch-Irish, filtered into the South and Appalachian districts of the country before 1800. The remaining 10 to 20 percent of these Irish Protestants probably converted to Protestantism after their arrival in this country—particularly in the South where the support of the Catholic Church was weakest.[11] Clearly, because the Census figures combine two groups with rather different ethnic experiences, it becomes important to know whether the Irish Protestants represent a separate ethnic subsociety, whether they have merged with the Irish Catholic subsociety, or whether they have simply disappeared as a distinct and self-conscious ethnic group.

While it is possible to visualize isolated sections of Appalachia where remnants of those Irish settlements described by travelers in the 1700s might still maintain a subculture and a sense of peoplehood based on a common experience of isolation and poverty, it is harder to visualize that Protestant Irish in other parts of the country would feel socially differentiated from their fellow Americans to the extent that they would have developed a subsociety within which most of their significant social interaction would occur, or that they would be bound by a distinctive sense of peoplehood. The denominational differences within Protestantism would by themselves have guaranteed that there would be relatively few common religious bonds with which to fortify a common historical identity. Nor does it seem probable that many would have become immersed in the Irish Catholic subsociety, unless through marriage or common concern for affairs in the homeland.

While it does not necessarily follow that they are not "real Irish Americans" simply because they are not perceived as such by Americans of other ethnic backgrounds, still, the most likely hypothesis regarding Protestant Irish as an ethnic group seems to be that, except for those few who may

[10] See Andrew Greeley, *Ethnicity, Denomination, and Inequality,* Sage Research Papers in the Social Sciences, Series No. 90-029, Vol. 4 (Beverly Hills: Sage Publications, 1976), p. 44. Here Greeley reports that Irish Catholics make up 3.4 percent of the national population and Irish Protestants 5.5 percent, based on a NORC Composite Sample of nearly 18,000.

[11] *Ibid.,* p. 78.

have recently immigrated, there is little tendency to regard themselves, or to be regarded, as a distinct ethnic group. We can probably safely conclude that unless they are specifically asked, the Protestant Irish do not think of themselves as Irish in any meaningful sense.[12] Because one measure of the survival of an ethnic subsociety is the preference for marriage within it, a rough test of the proposition that the Protestant Irish no longer exist as a self-conscious ethnic group would be the tendency to marry outside the Irish national origin group. The Census shows that the combined Catholic and Protestant Irish have the lowest percentage of endogamous marriages of any ethnic group—32 percent marry within their own national origin group, compared to 34 percent for Germans, 41 percent for Polish, 45 percent for English, and 53 percent for Italians.[13] On the other hand, Abramson's analysis in *Ethnic Diversity in Catholic America* showed that 43 percent of Irish Catholic males married endogamously.[14] Now if the Catholic Irish constitute roughly half of the Census' national origin group and have a higher percentage of endogamous marriages than the 32 percent indicated by the Census data, then clearly the Protestant Irish must have a lower percentage—perhaps as low as 22 percent. Ethnicity, among this group seems to have largely disappeared, so that in general the Protestant Irish can be said to have merged into American society at the social levels consistent with their socioeconomic accomplishments. This does not mean, however, that the Protestant Irish, as a statistical category, have no significance for our discussion of the Catholic Irish. In fact, in those studies where it is possible to measure the achievements of the two groups separately, such a comparison can help to clarify the status of the Irish Catholics with whom the Protestant Irish were combined in the Census report.

## IRISH CATHOLIC AND IRISH PROTESTANT ACHIEVEMENTS COMPARED

So pervasive has been the notion that Catholics do less well than Protestants in terms of education, income, and occupational prestige that the final unraveling of the meaning of the Census data comes as something of a surprise, for it now appears that it has been the Irish Catholics who have emerged as the super-achievers when compared either with Irish Protestants or with any other Protestant group. This new picture of the American Irish emerges from a composite sample of nearly 18,000 respondents, put together from 12 national surveys conducted by the National Opinion

[12] It is worth noting here that the Census question did not provide Scotch-Irish as a possible category for national origin, and did not provide for listing of multiple ethnic origins.

[13] U.S. Bureau of the Census, *Current Population Report,* Series P-20, No. 221, p. 7.

[14] Abramson, *Ethnic Diversity in Catholic America,* p. 53.

Research Center (NORC) in the late 1960s and 1970s, and reported by Andrew Greeley in *Ethnicity, Denomination, and Inequality.* "SuperNORC," as the composite sample is called, provides the best vehicle to date for interpreting the Census findings and for analyzing the separate achievements of Catholic and Protestant Irish. A brief consideration of their points of difference will show why the conclusions about Irish American status and social mobility might differ widely, depending on whether the focus is on national origins or on the socio-religious aspect of ethnicity.

When the Irish Catholic and Irish Protestant groups in the SuperNORC composite sample were compared with the national averages for education, occupational prestige, and family income, it became apparent that Irish Catholics consistently ranked above, and Irish Protestants below, the national averages. Moreover, Irish Catholics were above all other white Gentile ethnic groups in education and income, and were only marginally below the top-ranking British Protestants in occupational prestige.[15] (See Table 3.)

*TABLE 3*

*EDUCATION, OCCUPATIONAL PRESTIGE, AND INCOME FOR IRISH CATHOLICS, IRISH PROTESTANTS, AND BRITISH PROTESTANTS (NORC COMPOSITE SAMPLE*)*

| Ethnic Group | Years of Education (Mean) | Occupational Prestige of Head of Household (0–99) | Average Family Income (1974 dollars) |
|---|---|---|---|
| Irish Catholics | 12.5 | 43.7 | 12,426 |
| Irish Protestants | 10.9 | 36.7 | 9,147 |
| British Protestants | 12.4 | 43.9 | 10,354 |
| National Average | 11.5 | 41.8 | 10,623 |

Source: Compiled from Andrew Greeley, *Ethnicity, Denomination, and Inequality,* Sage Research Papers in the Social Sciences, Series No. 90-029, Vol. 4 (Beverly Hills: Sage Publications, 1976) pp. 45, 50, 53.

* The 12 national surveys included in the NORC composite sample were conducted in the late 1960s and 1970s.

Recalling that John Maguire, in 1868, had warned his countrymen of the evils of city life, and had lamented "the pernicious tendency of the Irish peasant to adopt a mode of livelihood for which he is not suited by previous knowledge or training," we can only conclude that Maguire underestimated the capacity of the Irish peasant, and of his descendants, to adapt to an urban life style. Today as many as 70 percent live in metropolitan regions outside the South, and over 60 percent continue to live in the six states of New England and the three states of the Middle Atlantic.[16]

[15] Jews, by definition, were not included in the comparisons of Gentile white ethnic groups, but for the record they scored ahead of all Gentile groups included in the study.

[16] Abramson, *Ethnic Diversity in Catholic America,* p. 29.

Though their forced adaptation to urban life had been difficult, they had never run the risk of being trapped in rural poverty. They had experienced enough of that in Ireland.

The Irish Protestants, on the other hand, present quite another picture. Having arrived earlier, many had chosen to settle the frontiers where their period of adjustment in the early years may well have been less socially traumatic, but where they later suffered the handicaps of isolation. The Appalachian Mountain valleys could not, at any period in history, compare with the stimulation, the challenge, and the occupational opportunity of New York, Philadelphia, and other cities of the eastern seaboard. While the Protestant Irish seemed favored in the early years of settlement, and did in fact provide outstanding leaders (whose descendants may have ceased even to identify with the Irish national origin group), the descendants of others among them are only now making a belated adaptation to urban America in such industrial centers as Detroit.

Although only 31 percent of those who identify as Protestant Irish currently live in metropolitan areas outside the South, the Detroit Area Study (using a 1966 probability sample which included 6 percent Catholic and 7 percent Protestant Irish) graphically portrayed the socioeconomic differences between Catholic and Protestant Irish males for this industrial center which has drawn so many unskilled workers from the rural South.[17] Considered as a national origin group, the Irish in this study ranked below the sample average in education, occupational status, and income, but when the Catholic Irish were considered separately they had achieved well above the sample average on all counts. Although the Protestant Irish received no separate treatment in the Detroit Area Study, their relatively low achievement is apparent when we consider the impact on the Catholic averages after the Protestant Irish are included. For the Catholic Irish, the mean occupational status was 56.9, but when the total Irish group was pooled it dropped to 43.8; for education it was 12.7 and dropped to 11.9, and for income it was $12,054 and dropped to $9,722.[18]

In light of the success demonstrated by the Irish Catholics as a group, it seems almost ironic that William Shannon—pondering the vast amount of talent that had been absorbed by the Catholic Church rather than entering society at large—should have written in 1976, "A cynic might speculate that if the Irish had been Unitarians, there would be no telling what worldly heights they might have scaled."[19] As for worldly heights, the Irish Catholics are scaling them better than almost anyone supposed, but, as Andrew Greeley points out, "A dream doesn't come true in its fullest sense

[17] Edward O. Laumann, *Bonds of Pluralism: The Form and Substance of Urban Social Networks* (New York: John Wiley and Sons, 1973), Ch. 3.

[18] *Ibid.,* pp. 46 and 60.

[19] William Shannon, "The Lasting Hurrah," *The New York Times Magazine,* March 14, 1976, p. 11.

until others admit it, and you are able to admit to yourself that it has come true. This ultimate approval has not yet been conceded to the Catholic ethnics."[20] Because the dominant group creates and upholds a mythology to sustain its own position, the "ultimate approval" is hard to earn. A hypothesis shot down by a fact is, however reluctantly, accepted as a dead hypothesis; but a myth shot down by a fact frequently lives on to breed still more erroneous conclusions.

The erroneous conclusions with which this discussion of Irish American achievement began can now be set straight, for the assumptions on which they were based have finally been challenged.

1. Irish Americans are not all Catholics. (As many as half of those who claim Irish origin are Protestant.)

2. Catholics in America are not necessarily lower in accomplishment than Protestants. (They vary greatly in their achievements, depending on their ethnic experiences and length of settlement in this country.)

3. Irish Catholics have been successful. (It would be as valid to attribute their success to their religion as it was to attribute their presumed failure to the same cause.)

In short, Irish Catholics as a group have done very well indeed in their century and more of American life, in spite of dire predictions to the contrary. It now remains our task to consider briefly the variations to be found within the larger group.

## VARIATIONS AMONG IRISH AMERICANS

Because the group averages we have so far been considering are statistical generalizations, they tend to disguise the variations to be found within an ethnic group, and to imply a homogeneity that rarely exists even among people who share a common heritage. Such variations take the form of region of settlement, rural or urban residence, or number of generations in America. When income, education, and occupation can be measured, social class variations within the group emerge to provide a reminder that social class is as important a determiner of life style as ethnic identity and that the Irish laborer may be as far removed from the Irish professional in the same city as are the inhabitants of two different regions. Since the social space—or *ethclass*—defined by the intersection of ethnic group with social class promotes primary ties which frequently remain within the familiar social class segment of the ethnic group, it follows that styles of behavior and ways of thinking are at least as decisively influenced by social class as by ethnic background.[21]

[20] Greeley, *Ethnicity, Denomination, and Inequality,* pp. 62–63.

[21] For an elaboration of the concept *ethclass* see Milton Gordon, *Assimilation in American Life* (New York: Oxford University Press, 1964), pp. 51–54.

Sociologists of the 1940s believed, by and large, that similarity of class interests would eventually predominate over any sense of ethnic identity and that people of like socioeconomic status would cross ethnic lines to share their social worlds. These early theorists failed to recognize that, at least in the established communities where the majority of the Irish had settled, ethnic social worlds often remained separate. Thus, if the Irish laborer and professional were moving in different social class worlds, they were nonetheless moving within one and the same ethnic subsociety, a proposition that undoubtedly applied to members of other ethnic subsocieties. As early as the 1950s, however, Milton Gordon questioned the assumption that "ethnic minorities not based on race [would], within any foreseeable period of time, decline virtually to the vanishing point." As he suggested then:

> in the larger cities and metropolitan areas, upper-middle class and even upper class ethnics are so numerous that they can and do develop their own social systems of primary and associational relationships within the ethnic framework. Furthermore such a process may develop even in the smaller cities as large numbers of ethnics move into the upper-middle class. In fact, the ability of ethnic groups in America to develop and maintain their own subsystems at all class levels is one of the most important sociological phenomena of American life.[22]

As Gordon has argued, if national origin or religion serves to prevent significant primary group contacts outside the ethnic group, those who are upwardly mobile have no alternative but to create their own social organizations, which reflect values and interests consistent with their new social class level, while remaining structurally separate from an equivalent status level in the host society. And more important still, the ability and/or desire to maintain such subsystems, even after discrimination has become a thing of the past, suggests that assimilation into the larger society need not be an automatic or inevitable choice.

Although many simply assume that the Irish have abandoned their ethnic identity and that their merger with Anglo-American society is a fait accompli, the research that would actually have documented the dismantling of the Irish American subsocieties at one or more class levels has been sketchy. It may even be that adequate research will never be done, unless by historians at some future time, since more volatile intergroup relations have drawn sociological attention away from those ethnic groups which seem so successfully to have overcome their initial handicaps. Nevertheless, in analyzing the variations among Irish Americans today, we can look for evidence to show whether or not a merging has actually occurred, and if so, under what circumstances and at what social levels.

[22] Milton M. Gordon, *Social Class in American Sociology* (Durham, N.C.:Duke University Press, 1958), pp. 119-20.

## REGIONAL, RURAL/URBAN, AND GENERATIONAL VARIATIONS

Unlike the Protestant Irish, whose apparent merging with the Anglo American Protestant society has been discussed earlier, the Catholic Irish developed a visible ethnic subsociety in communities where they settled in large numbers. Abramson, whose analysis of a 1964 national probability sample of American Catholics provides an estimate of 22 percent of Irish Catholics living in New England, 39 percent in the Middle Atlantic states, and another 18 percent living in the Northeastern Central states, with only 21 percent scattered through other parts of the country, concluded that the Irish were "characteristically and visibly, Easterners."[23] Lawrence McCaffrey, however, has made the point that too much emphasis may have been placed on the Irish experience in New England, in particular, to the neglect of the Irish in other parts of the United States where they merged more quickly into less structured societies. He points out that:

> When they moved into areas where the social structure was more flexible, varied, and dynamic than it was in New England, the Irish quickly took advantage of opportunities to improve their status. Outside New England, the Irish participated in the optimism and enthusiasm of an expanding nation, losing the defeatist attitudes that plagued them in places like Boston and Newburyport. Newly-arrived Irish immigrants who stayed out of New England were more likely to do well in the United States than third- or fourth-generation Boston Irishmen. In the Mid-Atlantic states and in the Midwest and West, they lived with and competed against Anglo-American Protestants and members of other ethnic groups, and the farther west the Irish went, the more confident and competitive they became.[24]

This is not to say, of course, that the Irish experienced no problems outside New England. Flaming crosses appeared on the front lawns of the socially mobile group aiming for the Philadelphia suburbs in the 1920s,[25] and Irish professionals were still unwelcome in elite men's clubs of the Midwest in the 1940s.[26] But those who remained in the East—particularly in New England—clearly found themselves interacting with an established and aloof Anglo Protestant majority. Stephen Birmingham, whose *Real Lace* describes the rise in fortune and the social lives of the "First Irish Families," observes that although the Irish had by 1973 made social inroads even in Boston, such that they had begun to be included on the boards of directors of prestigious banks, corporations, museums, and hospitals, it was

[23] Abramson, *Ethnic Diversity in Catholic America,* p. 30.

[24] Lawrence J. McCaffrey, *The Irish Diaspora in America,* (Bloomington: Indiana University Press, 1976), p. 79.

[25] Dennis Clark, *The Irish in Philadelphia: Ten Generations of Urban Experience* (Philadelphia: Temple University Press, 1974), p. 154.

[26] A. B. Hollingshead, *Elmtown's Youth* (New York: John Wiley and Sons, 1949), p. 63.

still to their advantage if they had come from outside New England—from New York or California, by way of a correct New England prep school and Yale—rather than coming from Dorchester by way of Boston College.[27]

National studies do not normally identify enough Irish Catholics to make possible precise comparisons by region of the country, but the NORC composite sample of close to 18,000 people provided enough data to indicate that while Irish Catholics have the highest average education and income of any Gentile group in the country as a whole, "in cities in the North, British Protestants have a higher rate of occupational mobility than do Irish Catholics—they get higher prestige jobs than do Irish Catholics with the same education."[28] Some differential between North and South is clearly present, but data are not available to document the apparent regional differential between East and West. Without such data, we can only say that the rigidity of the Yankee social structure in the East—particularly in New England—made social mobility more difficult and more time-consuming for those Irish who remained there in the early years, and that the effects may still persist.

In addition to being characteristically and visibly Easterners, Irish Catholics are characteristically urban and can lay claim to being at least third-generation Americans. Abramson found that nearly half were born in cities of over 500,000 or in suburbs of those cities, with another 29 percent born in smaller cities and only 25 percent born in small towns or in the country.[29] Thus, the move from a rural folk society in Ireland to an urban industrial society in America was not a temporary adaptation necessitated by external circumstances, but apparently the result of a conscious choice of urban life style—part of what Robert Kennedy described as the general demographic trend from rural to urban lives which happened to cross international boundaries, and which had as its goal the raising of the standard of living and the social position of those who emigrated.[30] The NORC composite sample indicates that Irish Catholics in all metropolitan regions outside the South, as well as in cities of over 2,000,000, maintain the economic advantage they hold over all other Gentile ethnic groups at the national level.[31] In other words, they have achieved these high average income levels in precisely those kinds of urban settings that they were so ill-prepared to deal with on their arrival in America.

In terms of length of residence in this country, Abramson found that, in 1964, 69 percent were in their third, or later, generation in this country, with both parents and up to all four grandparents born here; another 25

[27] Stephen Birmingham, *Real Lace: America's Irish Rich* (New York: Harper & Row, 1973), p. 282.

[28] Greeley, *Ethnicity, Denomination, and Inequality*, p. 54.

[29] Abramson, *Ethnic Diversity in Catholic America*, p. 34.

[30] Robert E. Kennedy, Jr., *The Irish: Emigration, Marriage, and Fertility* (Berkeley: University of California Press, 1973), p. 73.

[31] Greeley, *Ethnicity, Denomination, and Inequality*, p. 53.

percent were in the second generation, with one or both parents foreign-born; only 6 percent were of Irish birth themselves.[32] Nationally, 66 percent of male respondents were in white collar occupations, compared with 38 percent of their fathers; similarly, in terms of educational achievement, 49 percent of the sons had some experience with higher education compared with 15 percent of their fathers.[33]

A similar pattern emerged in Abramson's analysis of the Irish Catholics in Connecticut's three largest cities—New Haven, Hartford, and Bridgeport—which showed that, in the 1960s, the highest concentrations of both first- and second-generation Irish were in middle status occupations (40 percent and 37 percent, respectively), whereas the highest concentration of third, or later, generation Irish were in high status occupations (49 percent.)[34] Thus, the advantages of long residence are borne out in group averages. Long residence does not, however, guarantee upward mobility. Of more importance than the sheer length of time in America, apparently, is the ability to make the most of parental achievements in winning future status improvements. In his analysis of the NORC composite sample, Greeley indicates that "the most occupationally mobile groups (those likely to make the most of parental education and their own education in the occupational market) are the Polish, Irish Catholics, and German Catholics, while the Irish Protestants, the Scandinavian Protestants, and the American Protestants do least well."[35]

The ever increasing proportion of Irish who achieve higher status levels than their parents from one generation to the next is not in dispute—actually it follows the pattern originally noted for Newburyport. However, it is obvious that if as many as 66 percent are in white collar occupations nationally, then 34 percent are still in blue collar occupations; if 49 percent have some experience with higher education, then 51 percent still have only a high school education, or less. The fact that Irish Catholics have the highest *average* educational and income levels of any Gentile ethnic group does not, in other words, mean that all Irish are fractionally better educated or have higher income levels than all members of other Gentile groups.

The differences in experience and life style between low status and high status Irish Americans may, indeed, provide variations that are more significant than the variables of region, rural/urban settlement, or generation in America. Unfortunately, when we attempt to delineate the characteristics of the American Irish in terms of social class levels, hard data are scarce. We are forced to depend partly on impressionistic material in trying

[32] Abramson, *Ethnic Diversity in Catholic America,* p. 26.

[33] *Ibid.,* p. 41.

[34] Harold J. Abramson, "Ethnic Diversity in Three Connecticut Cities: Preliminary Findings" (Storrs: Ethnic Heritage Project: The Peoples of Connecticut, 1976), Table 14.

[35] Greeley, *Ethnicity, Denomination, and Inequality,* p. 50.

to determine whether or not an Irish American subsociety still exists at one or more class levels, and whether those at the upper status levels have, as predicted in the 1940s, found that, after a period of marginality, their class interests have superseded ethnic interests to promote a merging of upper-middle- or upper-class Irish Catholics with those at equivalent social class levels in the Anglo Protestant society.

## SOCIAL CLASS VARIATIONS

The 34 percent of Irish Catholic respondents in the national sample who remained in blue collar occupations—a category in the analysis which included not only craftsmen and factory operatives but also unskilled and semi-skilled labor—had clearly not "arrived" in any noteworthy sense, although they may, of course, have improved on their fathers' positions. A long-time resident of the Boston area who had grown up in the Irish-American community there observed recently in a private conversation:

> What about the present-day "ethnic Irish" found in such working-class areas as South Boston, Charlestown, and Brighton? The Irish in Boston have one of the lowest income levels of any group in the city. The ethnic Irish have not been fully assimilated there, and I have a feeling that these Irish are as much the "unmeltable ethnics" as Michael Novak's Polish.[36]

According to the Boston Area Survey data for the city of Boston in 1968, the Irish, with a median income of $5,000, were less well off financially than any ethnic group in the city except for Puerto Ricans, who had a median income of $3,700. By comparison, the median income for the city was $6,800, for Italians it was $7,000, and for blacks it was $7,500.[37]

Boston does not have a monopoly on working-class neighborhoods, but South Boston—because it is an old and conspicuously Irish section of Boston that reacted with bitterness and violence during the 1970s to court-ordered busing of students to its South Boston High School from the neighboring black community of Roxbury—has come to symbolize the tenacity with which the non-mobile Irish have clung to their familiar neighborhoods and resisted any efforts from the outside to change them. McCaffrey refers to the Irish of South Boston as "one obvious exception to the successful assimilation of Irish-Americans" and regards them as the "exception rather than the rule."[38] But the Irish who remain in communities like South Boston, Charlestown, Brighton, and other working-class areas do exist. The strength of their resistance to infiltration or change

[36] John F. Mulcahey, who was for 20 years with Massachusetts correctional agencies headquartered in Boston, in a private conversation, May 1977.

[37] Boston Area Survey, 1969, for 1968 (City Data), quoted in *The Boston Globe,* April 13, 1972, p. 3.

[38] McCaffrey, *The Irish Diaspora in America,* p. 188.

reflects the importance they attribute to the neighborhood as a symbol of the subsociety with which they identify.

David Matza, in a discussion of a group phenomenon which he terms "the disreputable poor," has described the process by which those who are non-mobile in an ethnic group gradually discover, like the Irish in South Boston, that they have somehow been left behind:

> The period during which newcomers enjoy relatively high morale is the temporal context within which the general factors favoring social mobility flourish. Its length varies, but the limits may be suggested. Demoralization may be avoided until newcomers are reduced to dregs, and the reduction of newcomers to dregs occurs when the steady desertion of mobile ethnic brethren is dramatically climaxed by an ecological invasion of new bands of ethnic or regional newcomers. When newcomers to the milieu of disreputable poverty predominate as neighbors and workmates, the remnants of earlier cohorts resentfully begin to notice what they have finally come to. They must now live and work with "them," and suddenly the previously obscure relation between their lot and that of their more fortunate or successful brethren from the original cohort is clear.[39]

The Irish of South Boston seem to have passed beyond the period of high morale and to have entered the period of demoralization, but they do not want to become either "disreputable poor" or "dregs." A tightly knit defense of the familiar ethnic neighborhood may appear to be all that stands between them and such a fate. To the extent that they are representative of other working-class, or lower-class, Irish neighborhoods in other areas, there is little to suggest that those who have been unable to achieve upward social mobility will accommodate easily to merging with others at their own status level for, as Matza points out, this would mean merging with "them."

Abramson's study of ethnic groups in Connecticut's three largest cities provides a view of the thinking and behavior of those Irish who are more characteristically middle class than the residents of South Boston. The Connecticut sample interviewed in the 1960s was evenly divided between blue collar and white collar workers, and, taking into account all generations, 40 percent were classified as middle class on the basis of occupation, income, and educational attainment. Thirty-eight percent, compared with 31 percent nationally, were first- or second-generation Irish, and the sons showed a smaller educational advantage over their fathers than was true for the national sample.[40] While others had moved to suburban areas, these Irish had remained urban dwellers. By comparing their responses to a series of questions related to their neighborhoods, friendships, and associational memberships with those of Anglo-Saxon Protes-

[39] David Matza, "The Disreputable Poor," in Reinhard Bendix and Seymour M. Lipset (eds.), *Class, Status, and Power,* 2nd ed. (New York: The Free Press, 1966), p. 301.

[40] Abramson, "Ethnic Diversity in Three Connecticut Cities," Table 13.

tants and Italians (a later-arriving, but larger group in Connecticut cities), a pattern of urban life emerges (see Table 4).

*TABLE 4*

*ANGLO-SAXON PROTESTANT, IRISH, AND ITALIAN CHARACTERISTICS IN THREE CONNECTICUT CITIES (1965)*

| Characteristic | Ethnic Group | | |
|---|---|---|---|
| | Anglo-Saxon Protestant | Irish | Italian |
| Owns or is buying home | 24% | 27% | 52% |
| Thinks of neighborhood as "true home" | 62 | 66 | 74 |
| Feels neighborhood is intimate | 23 | 23 | 32 |
| Visits with neighbors once a week or more | 39 | 37 | 39 |
| Neighbors include two or more close personal friends | 30 | 31 | 40 |
| Knows neighbors well enough to say "hello" | 50 | 65 | 69 |
| Visits with relatives once a week or more | 38 | 51 | 66 |
| Belongs to two or more voluntary associations | 27 | 36 | 24 |
| Member of a church | 65 | 90 | 89 |
| Attends church at least three or four times monthly | 35 | 79 | 63 |
| Political affiliation is Democrat | 27 | 56 | 58 |

Source: Harold J. Abramson, "Ethnic Diversity in Three Connecticut Cities: Preliminary Findings" (Storrs: Ethnic Heritage Project: The Peoples of Connecticut, 1976), Tables 16–26.

The Irish fall between the Anglo-Saxon Protestants and the Italians in all characteristics except those having to do with the amount of neighborhood visiting and the number of associational ties. They are more likely to belong to two or more voluntary associations, more likely to be members of a church, and more likely to attend regularly than either Anglo-Saxon Protestants or Italians. Clearly, in Connecticut's three largest cities, the Irish have stronger ties with their neighborhoods than do the Anglo-Saxon Protestants, but weaker ties than do the Italians. On the other hand, the Irish have associational ties—especially with their churches—which they might be reluctant to give up by moving to suburban areas.

Since there is no way of knowing from this particular study whether the friendships other than with relatives are selected from among those who are also of Irish background, or whether the non-church associational ties are related to ethnic interests, we can only surmise that these neighborhoods are in transition from the Irish enclaves that existed in these cities during the early part of this century to more ethnically mixed neighborhoods, and that, for the majority of those who remain, the strength of purely ethnic ties has weakened considerably. Yet the degree of assimilation with those of different ethnic backgrounds but similar status levels might be limited by the high level of church membership and attendance that the Irish indicate in this survey. However, there is no question to test the proposition that the Irish are either forced, or choose, to maintain an ethnic community into the future. Other than their associational and church ties, they appear to have only slightly more attachment to their neighborhoods than the Anglo-Saxon Protestants, and considerably less than the Italians. It seems probable that, except for the newest immigrants and the oldest Irish members of the community, they are merging into the activities of the wider society.

For the 9 percent of Irish nationally who now occupy positions at the upper-middle- and upper-class status levels,[41] movement to the suburbs has been a necessary accompaniment of this upward social mobility. Part of the appeal of upper-middle-class suburbs for the socially mobile may be precisely the fact that social class characteristics, rather than ethnic characteristics, form the basis of neighborhood ties. An interviewer in the Oral History Project for the Peoples of Connecticut study, when asked about the characteristics of those upper-middle-class Irish he had interviewed, stated:

> I found that at the lower social class levels people frequently thought of themselves as Irish and talked about it comfortably. At the professional level, more people tended to think of themselves as lawyers, or teachers, or businessmen, or whatever, and being Irish was not of particular importance to them. Some of them seemed surprised, at first, to be talking about it.[42]

Since the majority of upper-middle-class Americans have been socially mobile upward—some 60 percent having begun life at a lower social level—and since their occupations normally put them in contact with others whose interests crosscut ethnic lines, it would seem that the physical break with the ethnic neighborhood and the movement to suburban areas is the key to establishing a social break with an Irish ethnic identity. Few Catholic churches in suburban areas have ethnic histories and fewer children attend parochial schools. The upper-middle-class individual has been described as a person with a deliberate lack of interest in the past—a person oriented toward tomorrow rather than yesterday. Particularly among intellectuals, who will be discussed in Chapter 9, ethnic boundaries tend to evaporate. Without statistical evidence, it is impossible to say whether the Irish have followed the upper-middle-class pattern just described, but it seems highly likely that, if they so choose, there is nothing to stop them. Clearly, those who have "arrived" are hardly likely to focus on ethnic boundaries for the Irish when many are deliberately trying to eliminate boundaries for themselves.

[41] Greeley, *Ethnicity, Denomination and Inequality,* p. 59.

[42] Private conversation with Oral History Project interviewer, Matthew Magda, August 1976.

A young upper-middle class Irish American woman whose grandparents still lived in an Irish neighborhood in Boston made the following comment about her own family:

> My father founded a business with two Jewish partners, my mother writes books and doesn't socialize much, we don't go to the Catholic Church much, and I date a Protestant boy. My parents do have some Irish friends, but that's because they were in college with my father and Boston College was an Irish Catholic college when he went. They aren't friends because they're Irish, though, but because he knew them in college. It just happened that way.[43]

The position of the upper-middle class is somewhat ambiguous, as the young woman clearly implied, for sometimes it does "just happen that way" that one's friends are of Irish background—especially if one went to a Catholic college or is active in the Catholic Church—but at the same time it is viewed as more or less accidental and certainly not to be made much of. With increasing numbers of younger suburban-born Irish attending public rather than parochial schools, it may be that in the future it will not even "happen that way" that one's friends are either Irish or even Catholic. At the upper-middle class level, the option is clearly there for merging with social equals of non-Irish or non-Catholic background. With the possible exception of old—especially New England—communities, it appears likely that the merging has occurred.

If the upper-middle class focuses deliberately on the future, the upper class can afford to focus some of its attention on the past, since the fortunes usually were made long enough ago so that several generations may have had the advantages of careful elite schooling and proper presentation to "society." But the preoccupation with the past which has sometimes characterized the Anglo-American upper class has not been typical for the Irish. John Corry, who discusses the Irish upper class in "Golden Clan," says that "the American Irish seldom look back on their pasts, while the rich and social among them have looked back not at all."[44] This may change, but for those Irish who reached upper-class levels in the 1920s and whose grandchildren are now beginning to abandon the Irish Catholic society that was created in the intervening years, the past was less impressive than the present. Corry tells us that:

> When the Irish Catholics tried to move from the middle to the upper classes they found that the people who were there before them did not like it. The rich Irish Catholics formed a separate society, and among the most prominent of its bulwarks were the Murrays and McConnells. Their patriarch was Thomas E. Murray, the inventor and engineer, who died in 1929, and who left seven children to carry on his tradition of propriety and piety.

[43] Fallows, private interview, 1977.
[44] John Corry, "Golden Clan," *The New York Times Magazine,* March 13, 1977, p. 16.

> This they did, and had many children of their own, and it was these children who moved from a wholly Irish Catholic world into a more homogenized one. The old Irish Catholic society is no more.[45]

The old Irish Catholic society which Corry pronounces dead was very much alive through many decades of this century, however, and its parallel institutions still exist for those who wish to use them. They came about because the upper-class Anglo community was as defensive about protecting its status from incursions by the nouveaux riches as the South Boston Irish have been about protecting their cultural identity. Merging across ethnic lines, like movement from one social class level to the next, involves acceptance by those who are already there. Prestige, as the socially mobile inevitably discover, is accorded—not demanded or bought.

It is, moreover, a commonplace of social status studies that each group tends to define its own prestige in terms of its strengths, while it defines the prestige of others in terms of their apparent weaknesses. Additionally, the basis of prestige varies from group to group. For the Irish, the strength of their loyalty to the Catholic Church, and the fact that they often viewed themselves as better practicing Catholics than others, were sources of pride even during the years when their material accomplishments were few. Some of the brightest minds, some of the best executive skills, were in the service of the Church and of the vast structure of schools, hospitals, and other organizations it administered. Within the Catholic reference group, the high level of talent and piety displayed by the Irish in this extensive organizational network was a source of justifiable honor. But because it was structurally separate from the Protestant world, it earned no special credits there.

For upper-class Irish, the period of structural separation from the Protestant upper-class world involved the creation of their own Catholic charities for philanthropy and social activity, the establishment of Catholic debutante balls for girls being presented to Catholic society, the founding of elite Catholic schools and colleges, and the establishment of exclusive residential and resort areas.[46] Although some "old" Catholic families of English, Irish, and French descent had already joined the American upper class before the onslaught of the famine Irish, the rise to wealth of the later-arriving Irish Catholics foreshadowed a situation in which not only they, but perhaps also the Catholic ethnics of other backgrounds, would seek admission to Anglo-American upper-class society. Stephen Birmingham comments:

> Because of the purity of their faith, the wealthy Irish Catholics saw no reason why they should not be accepted by the highest of high Protestant so-

[45] *Ibid.*

[46] See Birmingham, *Real Lace,* Chs. 20 and 21; Corry, "The Golden Clan"; and Gordon, *Assimilation in American Life,* pp. 210–213, for a discussion of upper-class Catholic associations.

> ciety, particularly when they had no intention of going so far as to marry into it. And such social institutions as the *Social Register* seem to have agreed with them. Early in their rise to affluence, the little black and red book began listing such New York families as the Murrays, McDonnells, Cuddihys, and Graces, and, in San Francisco, the Mackays, Fairs, and Floods. . . .[47]

In spite of all this, the Irish—the first large group of Catholics to produce candidates for upper-class status within their own subsociety—served their period of upper-class marginality in their own Catholic organizations. In New York, the Foundling Hospital was a favorite charity, the Catholic Big Sisters (the Catholic equivalent of the Junior League) served to bring young women together for charitable work and sociability, and the Papal Order of the Knights of Malta included the most aristocratic of the Catholic men. Catholic debutante balls—the Gotham Ball in New York and the St. Nicholas Cotillion in Boston—presented upper-middle- and upper-class girls to Catholic society. Elite Catholic boarding schools—Canterbury in New Milford, Connecticut, and Portsmouth Priory in Portsmouth, Rhode Island—prepared young men for Georgetown University, while girls attended schools operated by the Religious of the Sacred Heart and went from there to Barat in Lake Forest, Illinois, or to Manhattanville in Purchase, New York. Southhampton, and the "Irish Channel" on Long Island's opposite shore, became early upper-class Irish beachheads.

These institutions, schools, and resorts still remain, but the upper-class Irish who were instrumental in giving them their early luster now increasingly find them "second rate," and upwardly mobile Catholics of other ethnic backgrounds take their place. The debutante Gotham Ball is still supported by the upper-class Irish, and its proceeds still go to the New York Foundling Hospital, but, as Birmingham points out,

> if a girl comes out *only* at the Gotham, and nowhere else, she is not really considered "out" at all. . . . Much more exclusive and fashionable—and fun—were the Junior Assemblies and the Baltimore Cotillion . . . neither of which is Catholic, and if an Irish Catholic girl is invited to come out at one of these, she has really entered society in an important way.[48]

The network of social institutions developed by the Irish upper class during its rise to acceptance was almost as elitist as the Protestant society it paralleled—but not quite.

Corry points out that "the precise moment when the Irish Catholics passed truly into society is unclear, but it is almost certain that the place where it happened was Southhampton." In the smaller cities of America, where the established upper classes guarded their "society" with as much tenacity as did the Anglo-Americans in the great cities, World War I served

[47] Birmingham, *Real Lace.* p. 224.
[48] *Ibid.,* p. 230.

as the occasion for bringing together Irish Catholics and Protestants of various denominations and backgrounds. Upper-middle-class clubs were starting to include Irish members in the 1920s, elite country clubs in financial trouble passed the word that they would accept Irish members in the Depression years, and by the 1940s occasional marriages between Irish and Anglo-Americans of similar upper-class status signaled the beginning of the end of the marginal period.

As this chapter has demonstrated, the parallel Irish Catholic structures that developed out of necessity during the group's first surge of upward mobility functioned to separate their lives, at the primary level, from those of Anglo Protestants. The parallel institutions still exist, and are increasingly including Catholics from other ethnic backgrounds, but they appear to be of decreasing importance for the Irish themselves. Manhattanville College, long considered one of the most elite of upper-class colleges for women, is now coeducational and in 1977 enrolled approximately 13 percent Jewish students among the men, over 25 percent Protestants in the total student body, and only 64 percent Catholics—of whom relatively few were actively involved in religion. No longer an upper-class Irish Catholic women's college, Manhattanville has drawn fewer and fewer Irish women. The favored upper-class Irish Catholic choices for women are Wellesley, Smith and Vassar, and the Ivy League colleges are the goals of the men.[49]

If the Irish were the first large immigrant group to have tested the proposition that ethnic identity would no longer be of major significance to those who were entering their second, third, and later generations in this country and who had, as a group, entered the middle status levels, they appear to have proven its veracity. But in the process they have also shown that structural separation from Anglo Protestant society required the development of their own Catholic institutions at all class levels, and that these may remain as long as there are those who feel more comfortable in them, even after the necessity for them has passed.

[49] John D. Murray, Professor of Sociology at Manhattanville, in a private telephone conversation, August 1977.

# CHAPTER SIX

# *Self-Portraits of Irish Americans*

Those undergoing the pressures to assimilate may define events differently from those who merely observe the process, yet in many families of Irish ancestry the break with the past and the struggle to make a living in the new country have led to forgetfulness of what the events were really like. In some families an oral tradition has persisted, passed down from father to son and mother to daughter by people who felt their lives were too unexceptional to record in writing but who hoped they would, nevertheless, be remembered by someone. In other families a Bible recorded the births and deaths of the generations as each moved farther from an Irish past, until at length the old Bible was discarded in a careless gesture. In still other families the past was never known, for parents and children were separated before the words were spoken, adolescents struck out on their own without caring to hear, or the difficult past was shielded from children whose futures were meant to be brighter.

Although every family is different, when the Irish reminisce about their own, or their ancestors', efforts to make a new life in America, certain themes emerge recurrently. To the extent that these themes deal with the perplexities of the uprooted as they try to understand and make their way in a new country, they are universal immigrant themes. To the extent that they center specifically around the Irish past and the Irish Catholic neighborhoods and communal bonds in America, they capture those qualities which make each ethnic subculture unique. To the extent that they speak of the special problems of men or women, of rural or urban life, of failure or success, they suggest the diversity that makes an ethnic subsociety a social world within itself.

The self-portraits that comprise the bulk of this chapter are not case histories in the usual sense, but provide instead brief glimpses into the thinking of ordinary people who told of their families and recorded their thoughts with no expectation that their lives would be judged especially typical or atypical. The earliest of the interviews on which these self-portraits are based were made during the 1930s when, as part of the Works Progress Administration (WPA) *Federal Writers' Project on the Growth of Bridgeport, Connecticut,* members of the Irish community were asked to tell what they recalled of their early years in Ireland and America, and to discuss their current activities, attitudes, and hopes for the future. The remaining self-portraits are based on tape-recorded interviews in the 1970s, conducted by the author and by interviewers for the Peoples of Connecticut *Oral History Project* at the University of Connecticut. Taken together, they will explore the common themes of the Irish experience in America and will suggest the variety of responses to these themes, based upon different times of arrival, differences between men and women, differences in rural or urban residence, and differences in social class.

## LEAVING IRELAND BEHIND

The reasons for leaving home are always specific, even though the undercurrents of poverty, crop failure, lack of opportunity, and hope for adventure or a new start appear in nearly every account. Often the immigrants were young and single. Patrick, in the 1860s, fought with the landlord's son over a girl and, knowing that things would not go well with him if he remained in Ireland, headed for a boat to America the next morning. In time he became one of the few successful Irish farmers in a small Yankee village in western Massachusetts. Mary and her sister grew discouraged on their parents' subsistence farm, and in 1871 simply packed up and left to become domestics in wealthy New England homes where they had friends working. Annie, in 1880, already had three sisters and two brothers in America when she was sent the passage money to join them for what turned out to be a permanent visit. In 1890 Michael shocked his family by turning down the farm to which he was entitled as the eldest brother and joining his cousins in New York. Sometimes entire families came. During the 1850s, a father of nine decided to sell his respectable but unprofitable farm and convert his holdings into gold so he, like his brother before him, could buy a tract of farmland in Connecticut. A family of thirteen children accompanied their mother when she joined an aunt in America in the 1860s. Upon the death of her husband, this woman realized that the family could no longer continue their pleasant existence as caretakers on the estate her husband had managed for an English lord.

## I ENTERED AMERICA SAD AT HEART

Mrs. O, who had lived in America for thirty years when she was first interviewed in the 1930s, is representative of the young Irish women who, although they had emigrated reluctantly, still made lives as respected members of communities in Eastern cities after the turn of the Century.[1]

"I was born in Limerick, County Munster, on the River Shannon, in 1880. This is in the southern part of Ireland where we are noted for our beautiful scenery and our wonderful green pastures where the cattle graze.

[1] *WPA Federal Writers' Project on the Growth of Bridgeport, Connecticut* (Storrs: Ethnic Heritage Project: The Peoples of Connecticut, 1975), 1939 interview with Mrs. O.

The best firkins of butter that were ever made come from there, and practically all the best butter sold in England comes from Limerick. Our town was noted far and wide for its great fishing and hunting. Wonderful thoroughbred horses were raised there. We had crossroads dances held out in the country where the roads crossed. I can remember them as if it all happened yesterday. I only wish I could live those days over again. I was so happy. Then we had the old-fashioned kitchen dances held at neighbors' homes each night, with turns held so they would be in different homes each time. I never attended a public dance in my life.

"Schooling was limited to what the English government saw fit to give us. It was all very unfair. Girls and boys had to attend separate schools and no Gaelic was taught. Our teachers were Irish people, mostly from our village. Some way or other they had gotten a fair education, but their word was not taken for our marks. Once a year an examiner came from England to examine us one by one, then they marked us accordingly, which was unfair to our teachers and to us. I can remember in my early childhood the hatred of the English Protestant for the Irish Roman Catholic. In some districts, the Mass was held in dugouts, and all the police were English, maintained by the English government.[2] They were always known as "peelers" or "bobbies," and every town had a barrack where they made their headquarters. My only impression was that they lacked all the essentials that went to make for law and order, yet they made their livings at the expense of the Irish.

"Every Tuesday was market day, when all produce, cattle, and horses were brought to market in the center of the town. English merchants came over from England to buy, and they certainly took advantage of us. Here were prize cattle, grazed on the best pastures in Ireland, fed on the best grain, and then sold to the crafty Englishmen for whatever they offered us. The large firkins of butter that went for almost nothing were sold per pound in England for fancy prices. All their profits were made at our expense. Due to the suppression of the English, the Irish were practically driven from their homes. My two sisters came to America four years before I did, and I also had a brother here. They sent money home to my parents every month, and later they sent me my passage.

"I sailed for America on the old *Majestic.* I was so seasick, and there were many others the same way, but none of the members of the crew seemed to care whether we lived or died. The leaving home and parting with dear ones was sad enough, but to be so ill and have no loving care made it worse. I entered America sad at heart. Our boat came in a day earlier than it was expected, and there was no one there to meet me. Finally a Roman Catholic priest, an immigrant from Ireland, collected all the

[2] When Mrs. O was a child in Ireland, Mass was offered in prosperous churches, and the policemen were mostly Irish Catholics and not English, though they were working for the English. It is well to remember that Mrs. O, like many whose recollections have been passed down in Irish families, was a young girl when she left Ireland. Such recollections are true in spirit but frequently inaccurate in detail.

Catholics—40 in number—and took them to his rectory which was not far from Castle Garden, now known as Ellis Island.[3]

"I became panicky when my folks did not come. They finally arrived at noon the next day, but before the priest would let you go he first asked your people for a very exacting description of you, then he came back and asked the same question of you. This, he claimed, was because a beautiful Dublin girl had come to New York to an uncle she had never seen, and was taken away by the wrong person. The girl was never located, though her uncle searched for her. Before I was given to my people, the housekeeper came to me and said, 'If that is your brother with your sisters, you can be proud of him. He is a credit to Irish soil.'

"I was in New York working for a month when my sister married and moved to Bridgeport, Connecticut. I came with her and later worked for a family as a waitress. My sister's husband was very well known in Bridgeport, and we attended the many social functions held by the Irish immigrants there. At one of these I met my husband, who was an emigrant from Roscommon who had come to this country many years before I did, and only eight years after I came to America I was married."

## THOSE WERE DARK AND EVIL DAYS

Mr. D, an unmarried blue collar worker, had been in America over 40 years when he spoke in 1975 about his childhood in Ireland during the tumultuous period following the Easter Rebellion in 1916.[4] He had known at first hand the excitement and terror of the years before the formation of the Irish Free State. The improvidence of his father, along with the high taxes and rents paid to an absentee landlord, had kept the family impoverished, yet this one scholarly son had been singled out to be educated and to enter the priesthood.[5] He describes, in the words that follow, the events that led up to his emigration to America, his arrival at the start of the Depression, and his feeling of isolation.

"I was born in the west of Ireland, in 1911, in County Leitrim between a town called Drumshambo and a small village called Dowra. Ours was a farmhouse out in the country. There were all Catholics in that section and the priest, you might say, was the leader of the parish. There were

[3] Castle Garden served as an immigration station from 1855 to 1892, when Ellis Island was opened. Mrs. O must have been one of the last Irish immigrants to arrive at Castle Garden. Since she was born in 1880, this would have made her 12 years old at the time.

[4] *Oral History Project* (Storrs: Ethnic Heritage Project: The Peoples of Connecticut), 1975 interview with Mr. D.

[5] When Mr. D was a child, Irish farmers were mostly peasant proprietors. Beginning in the 1880s and ending in 1908, British government loans had converted tenant farmers into owners of the land they occupied. Since Mr. D vividly recalled letters to his father demanding back rent on their farm, his family may have been an exception.

dances once in a while, a football team, a concert once in a while, that's about all. I went to the National School, but at that time there was a breakdown in the government because this was the time of the trouble in Ireland, and of course the British government wasn't too concerned about the educational conditions. It was just after the 1916 Easter Rebellion and before Ireland had its independence.

"I remember one time in church, the door opened and English soldiers forced their way toward the altar in full battle gear, wearing helmets. And I remember the priest turned around and said that nobody should be afraid. "Let the Devil come forward," he said. Of course, it was quite exciting for us children, but I imagine the adults were really terrified. Something that always remained in my mind—we had to stay for church school, as you'd call it here, and I remember looking across to the other part of the church and seeing one of those same soldiers kneeling down praying. He was probably a Catholic, and when they had a break and the other soldiers went across the street to the public house he was kneeling here praying. He probably lived in terror too, never knew when his life would end, with all kinds of ambushes and so forth. It seemed so strange. It made the British seem human.

"A couple of days after that, the British came in over the mountains with armored cars, cavalry, planes, to surround our whole district. It was a 'round-up' that continued all day from 3 o'clock in the morning till 11 o'clock at night when they took all the men to a central field and had the R.I.C. (Irish police) sergeant point out the men they were looking for. But they didn't find anybody they wanted because the men had spies in Dublin Castle and knew exactly what was happening. I was ten years old then. Those were dark and evil days.

"A couple of days after the round-up, my parents decided to send me to live with a grand uncle who was a priest in another part of Ireland—in County Meath, about 100 miles from my home. I was to go to college to become a priest, but I had an aunt who was his housekeeper who had married into a family where there were six brothers who were involved in all this trouble and of course they were my heroes. Instead of teaching me to play handball or football they taught me how to throw hand grenades and conduct ambushes. I only became involved in all this because my aunt had married into this family, otherwise it would have just passed me by as it did so many other people. It's hard to say the effect it had on me. Children, just like in Belfast today, they don't know any different. Their whole world lives like that. They assume it's absolutely normal because they can't evaluate it against any other kind of life. But of course we were brought up in a very religious atmosphere and my grand-uncle was a man who loved poetry and reading, and he instilled that love in me.

"Finally my uncle was transferred back to the parish where I was born, so I went to school there again and helped on the family farm until I finished the tenth standard—that's about the equivalent of high school—and after that I worked on the farm for another five or six years, and finally went to live with my uncle. He wanted me to go to college, so he left me some money when he died. Instead of going to college, I came to America. I had cousins here, and one of them sponsored me.

"I thought it would be better in America, but I arrived on the edge of the Depression. I was willing to work hard, but I was out of work for two years, and I remember my people in Ireland had to send me money. Of course, I repaid it many times over, but during these years I did a lot of thinking about why conditions should be as they were, why I had come to this country. I was so bitterly disappointed that the system we lived under would deny me the opportunity to work. So I wondered how conditions could be improved. There was one system that did promise a utopia—Communism—but as it was put into practice in Russia it certainly seemed to me a brutal system. So I decided the best way to improve the lot of the working man was through unionism. They had a union in the water company where I finally found work, but not in the meter reading department where I was, so I was instrumental, with a few others, in bringing the union to the meter reading department. Naturally there was opposition, but you must stand up for what you believe in, and I believe in a good, strong, honest union. I think that is the hope of the working man.

"The union did make a difference in our living standard, but I might as well tell you I'm not much interested in material things. As long as I have enough money to buy food, a place to sleep, and what I like most in life—reading. Books are not too expensive, and I belong to the public library. The people I admire and look up to would be considered rebels: William Sloane Coffin, the Berrigan brothers, and Rabbi Goldberg here in H——. One reason I never got married, going through the horrible Depression and almost drowning to death myself, I couldn't see the responsibility of someone else. Probably many Irish couldn't understand my outlook on life, but I think the reason I feel as I do is my upbringing, my childhood, what I went through when I came to this country—they left a scar. I do identify with a revolutionary past, and there are others who must feel as I do, but I don't have contact with them except in books."

### TIES WITH THE IRISH SUBSOCIETY

The majority of Irish who came to America had been preceded by members of their families who had come earlier. They moved immediately into neighborhoods where other Irish people lived, and if they married they were likely to select a partner from the Irish community. The identity they established as members of this subsociety often failed to provide them with any significant bonds at the primary level outside it. During the 1850s Honora and her husband ran a small store for the Irish community that had gravitated to Lewiston, Maine, for work in the cotton bleacheries. While raising eleven children Honora both read and wrote letters for newly arrived immigrants and served as midwife when the occasion demanded it. Nellie, in the 1880s, ran a boarding house in Lawrence, Massachusetts, where young men working in construction and for the street railway company could find a touch of home in the Irish community before establishing families of their own.

## WE WERE ALWAYS TAUGHT TO BE PROUD

Mrs. S., whose second-generation Irish family had by the 1880s become prosperous in the Irish community of Bridgeport, Connecticut, described her family's continued reliance on the Irish community, even after they had physically moved out to Yankee neighborhoods.[6]

"At my grandfather's death, my father bought the property between Devitt's and Leverty's on Main Street at Bull's Head, where he brought his wife. Bull's Head was filled with Irish families who always seemed to gather together. The Yankees had nothing to do with them. I was born in 1869, and when we children were growing up my father bought a house on Lumber Street, a Yankee district. We saw very little of the Yankees when I was a child, and at school we were pointed out as "Irish paddies." All of my parents' friends and mine were Irish, as they still are. But we had a happy home life on Lumber Street. Relatives from everywhere came to visit us and we used to sing and dance to all the old Irish songs and ballads and dance the Irish jig. We were always taught to be proud of being Irish and Catholic, and we knew all the history and legends of Ireland and followed the happenings in Ireland as much as we did the local news.

"I was married from the Lumber Street house, and we went to live in a remodeled old-fashioned house at the corner of Washington and Park Avenues. There were no Irish families at that end of Washington Avenue then, only Yankees. It was two years before our neighbors spoke to us, but when we had a big fire our snootiest neighbor offered us rooms for the night. I enjoyed telling her we had several friends who would look after us.

"We had a farm in Stephey for the summer when our children were small. There were no Irish families there then either, and we saw only Yankees except on Sundays when our friends would come visiting. The Yankees were nice to us in that neighborhood, but they were never intimate with us. We used to visit back and forth, but they talked about us as though we were Negroes or Jews and the children overheard things that were unkind or prejudiced. I think they were polite to us because of my husband's business. He had worked for a hardware company since he left school, and he stayed with them until 1918, but even the people he worked for tried to keep him feeling inferior to them.

[6] *WPA Federal Writers' Project,* 1939 interview with Mrs. S.

"I often think that some of the Irish people who pretend not to be Irish and look down on their own kind are really ashamed of their background and ignorant of their heritage. My brother and sisters are now Protestants, and I know a woman, the daughter of an old Irish family which was well-to-do and respected, who scorns all the Irish, though she went to an Irish preparatory school and married an Irishman. She is society editor of one of the newspapers and tries not to print notices about Irish Catholic organizations, saying that the weddings don't leave enough space. I think it's a shame that there isn't an Irish organization of some kind that would keep alive the history and memory of our forefathers in America and in Ireland."

## THEY'RE NOT GOING BACK, SO THEY MUST BE PRETTY HAPPY HERE

Typical of the spirit of adventure that brought many younger sons to America in this century is the account provided by Mr. D, a middle-aged white collar worker who was interviewed in 1975.[7] He had been raised in a small village on Galway Bay and had worked on the family farm from the time he left school at fourteen until he decided to come to America at eighteen in 1947.

"There were five boys in our family and the farm was only enough to support one, so I began to realize that four of us would have to go somewhere, and I got a chance to come here. I didn't really have to leave because of need but at eighteen or nineteen most of the fellows growing up then wanted to go someplace. Everybody knew America was the best place. A lot of excitement attached to going to America. There was a cousin of mine with me when I came. We arrived in New York, and it was very exciting. I was met at the boat by my aunt from Hartford, and several aunts and uncles in New York, and some of their friends. We got the royal treatment. We stayed overnight with an uncle who'd lived in Brooklyn since 1895 and came to Hartford the next day. The first place I lived was with some family friends in a very nice neighborhood. I was really impressed with it.

"After coming to my aunt's I went to work for a department store and I found out you have to go by the clock, which is something you never did in Ireland except on Sunday going to church. But it didn't take me long to get used to it, and then later I went to work for an insurance company because of more money and better opportunities. I started in 1947 and I'm still there. That was about when the Irish-American Home Society was founded. It had mostly dances and social functions, such as Sunday night singalongs and that type of thing. There were less than 100 in it then—half and half Irish and Irish American. My wife is Irish American. I met her

[7] *Oral History Project,* 1975 interview with Mr. D.

there. Now the club has over 1,000 members and keeps getting more Irish Americans. It's a nonpolitical club with a Home we built about seven years ago with picnic grounds, a football field, an ample parking lot. We have dances, social functions; we charter busses to go to ball games; we have two charter flights going to Ireland in the summer; we have the local Gaelic football team that plays games at the club two or three times a month from May to September. We have what they call a Feis—a dancing competition—every summer for kids from ages four to twenty-one, and anywhere from 500 to 1,000 kids come from all over the area: New York, Boston.

"There's a definite effort to preserve the Irish heritage and keep the youth in touch with it through music and song. Then we have a weekly newspaper and two Irish radio programs every Sunday, where we can get hold of the Irish news. There's concern about the situation in Belfast, and I think people are very depressed about the whole thing. Ireland used to be such a peaceful place. It's hard to imagine all this going on there now. A lot of individuals are very concerned and some of them have raised money, but as a club we don't want to get involved in politics, American *or* Irish.

"When I became a voter in 1947 I was told by the old-timers back then that the Democratic Party was the best party for the working man, so I became a Democrat. But I soon found out that you vote for whoever you think is best for the office. All in all, I'd say the majority of the club members are Democrats. We've all been disappointed with the Watergate situation, all the Irish community, but if anything it has strengthened our faith in America, because it shows that even the President can't do wrong and get away with it. Most of the people I know find America fulfills their expectations. They're not going back, so they must be pretty happy here."

## BORN IN SAINT FANNAHAN'S WELL

The willingness to help fellow countrymen through patronage or simple goodwill—a valuable asset in the Irish subsociety—is revealed in this account by a successful third-generation Irish American who was in his seventies when he told, in 1968, about his own father's start in a lucrative real estate development career at the turn of the century.[8]

"My uncle Cornelius was in Attleboro, Massachusetts, working for a real estate development company called the Eastern Development and Realty Company when he kept writing to my father saying, 'Look, we can make money at this. Why don't you come down and try it out for at least a month?' And after some insistence from him, my father went to Attleboro. He looked at the property they were selling, and was given the job of ringing doorbells and distributing the usual flyers.

"So he went out on this very hot summer day in July or August, and he rang doorbells and he passed out flyers to try to get people interested,

[8] Fallows, private collection, 1968 interview with Mr. O.

and he wasn't doing very well. In the midst of this, he knocked at a door and a little Irish woman came to answer. He gave his name and said, 'We have some very fine land out here on ——— Street. I'd like to have you look at the plans, because it's going to develop very well.' Of course she said, 'I'm not interested at all,' but it was so hot he asked if he could have a drink of water. She thought it was just a sales trick, but she took him to the kitchen and after she'd gotten him the water she asked what part of Ireland his folks had come from.

"He told her they'd come from Tipperary, not far from Mitchelstown, but that she wouldn't know the place because it was just a crossroads.[9] She asked the name, and when he told her Saint Fannahan's Well she said, 'Glory be to God! I was born in Saint Fannahan's Well. Would you have a cup of tea, and what did you say your business was? Just starting in the real estate business? Well, let me have a look at what you have.' She bought four lots and she sold four more for him, and he never got out of the real estate business. The next year he became a participating partner, and the year after that he and his brother Cornelius bought out the three men who had run it. From there on they were both quite successful."

## TIES WITH IRELAND

For every family that has kept up significant ties with Ireland after three or more generations in America, there are countless more who have not. In the mid-1970s, the English Thames Production Company, in Boston to do a series on Irish immigration, broadcast a radio appeal to those of Irish ancestry to call and contribute whatever information they could about their immigrant past. Of those who called, few could remember, or had ever known, the specifics of their family histories—the counties their ancestors had come from, the year of arrival, their mothers' maiden names—yet all knew they had some connection with Ireland. Perhaps, for some, it was the first occasion they had had to realize how much had been forgotten.

### THE MEETING OF THE CLAN

One of the few who called the Thames Production Company with specific material on her family's history was a Boston woman who had started earlier to gather information about the Irish and American sides of her own Fitzgerald clan from Limerick. Through correspondence with a cousin in Ireland, she had become enthusiastic about the idea of bringing the two sides of the family together, and finally in 1970 the meeting had been ar-

[9] It had been this family's belief that their ancestral home was in Tipperary, but, some 130 years after the first pre-famine member of the family immigrated, a trip to Ireland in search of family roots turned up the unexpected discovery that Saint Fannahan's Well was just over the line from Tipperary and was in Cork.

ranged. Her niece, in 1975, discussed what it had been like for an upper-middle-class American girl to return to the family farm in Limerick and discover that her relatives were as happy in Ireland as she was in America.[10]

"I was only about fifteen in 1970 when the American contingent of our clan decided to go back to Limerick to visit Uncle Ned, the oldest surviving member of our family in Ireland. An older brother and sister of Uncle Ned's had emigrated to America in the late 1800s, and Ned and his brother Will had remained on the ancestral farm and married girls whose dowries had brought them lands adjoining what they inherited from their father. When we were there, one owned the largest dairy farm in Limerick and the other owned the largest creamery. My grandfather was the older brother who emigrated, and the 17 of us who descended on Uncle Ned were Grandfather's seven out of nine children and five grandchildren who now live all over the United States—in Oregon, Florida, Arizona, Connecticut, Massachusetts, Illinois and Washington, D. C. It was the first time the American and Irish cousins had all met. It was a real meeting of the clan.

"They really had a funny view of what we would be like, based on stories and movies, so my young Irish cousins really thought we would be a wild and rowdy bunch, wearing cowboy boots and carrying guns. Americans think of the Irish as wild and rowdy, but the Irish expected us to be that way and were really pleased that we weren't. The impression has persisted all these years. There must be environments in Ireland that can produce a rowdy radical too, just as in America, but while we're a little different from them it's not in conspicuous ways. They were calm, quiet, contented, good Catholics, with strong family ties and respect between brothers and sisters. Well behaved people. Whether going to parish schools has anything to do with it, I don't know.

"In my own American family we've talked a lot about what it is that a Catholic education provides. You should hear my father on the subject; he says it so well. I went to first grade in the town parochial school, then from second through sixth in public school, then to the Convent of the Sacred Heart from eighth through twelfth. My father just feels you don't get a religious, God-centered, Catholic education in public school. You don't get the same kind of Catholic ethics. Catechism once a week is pretty flimsy, as I remember it, and we didn't like it as much as having it taught in school. The main thing is to get the Catholic ethics, I think, and I feel I got that—a real knowledge of right and wrong. My brother went to a Catholic college and I'd have liked to go to the same one my father went to, but they just didn't have the program I wanted in psychobiology so I went to Vassar mainly because of its biopsychology program. That's definitely *not* a Catholic school, but the thing is I would have gone to one if they had the program I wanted. I really believe in religion—in God.

"Our relatives in Ireland were surprised to find out that we were as devout Catholics as they were. My father carries a rosary in his pocket all

[10] Fallows, private collection, 1975 interview with Miss C.

the time, and when they were questioning us about our religious commitment, he took out his rosary and showed it to Uncle Ned, who was really pleased to find out that this kind of Catholicism has carried over and not become as radical in America as they expected.

"It was a calming experience going back. By the end of our two weeks, we found ourselves speaking more softly. They are contented people. No one in our family has emigrated since 1899, and when my aunt asked an Irish cousin what his dreams in life were, he didn't talk about going to America or making money. If he could have one wish, he said, he would travel around Ireland and play his fiddle. They have a good life, and the mothers and children on the American side of the clan settled right in comfortably to life in the country. It was a real vacation. For the fathers it was a little different. They enjoyed the relaxation but knew their lives were in the fast-paced world of American business which they were used to. Perhaps there is something to the idea that the more adventurous were the ones that emigrated."

### THEY ARE JUST CHILDREN

While the warfare in Northern Ireland has captured the sympathy of some American Irish who support with money, if not with arms, the struggles of Catholics in Protestant Northern Ireland, there are other Irish Americans who see in the ancient resentments between Catholics and Protestants an image of tensions that they feel they have surmounted in America. Each summer since 1975, children from the most battle-torn sections of Belfast are flown to join receiving Protestant and Catholic families—most, but not all of them Irish—who have taken this way of demonstrating what the Irish American experience is all about. The Irish Protestant minister who initiated the plan of bringing Irish children to spend a summer in America explains:[11]

"I know that Protestant and Catholic clergy in Northern Ireland are working together to try to bring this fighting to an end, but the antagonisms run deep. But once the children leave their barricaded streets in Belfast and get on the plane for America, they are just children. Their summer in America has been paid for by donations from private people, from service organizations, and by Catholic and Protestant churches. It is a group effort. Like others who take part in this project with the children of Belfast, I know that Ireland really plays a small part in my life. But it has a big place in my heart."

### THE PLACE OF THE IRISH IN AMERICA

Like most Americans, the majority of Irish Americans see their lives in personal and private terms, but when asked what they feel lies ahead for themselves and for other Irish Americans they may speak in quite sweeping

[11] Fallows, private collection, 1976 interview with Mr. C.

terms. Some lament the loss of ethnic consciousness on the part of those around them; others feel that to be anything other than 100 percent American is ridiculous and contrived; still others identify with what their own segment of the Irish American community has experienced since its arrival here but feel no ties with Ireland itself. The majority feel that they have merged into American life and that both they and America are better for it.

## THE IRISHMAN NEVER FEELS THAT HE IS A FOREIGNER

An anonymous letter writer contributed the following appraisal of his countrymen's position and attitudes toward life in America, as part of the *Federal Writer's Project on the Growth of Bridgeport, Connecticut,* in 1939:[12]

"In the case of most foreign-born people, they usually are reluctant to admit to their own or their parents' foreign birth. For some reason they are of the opinion that such an admission, whether they are American citizens or not, detracts from their status as a citizen. The foreign-born Irishman is proud of his birthright, as is the second generation proud that their parents were born on the 'ould sod.' While other nationalities look with envy upon their countrymen who were fortunate enough to be born in this country, the Irishman born in his native land looks upon the American-born as though he had missed something by not being born in Ireland. The Irishman never feels that he is a foreigner. While other Europeans spend years becoming Americans, the Irishman feels he is American in a matter of weeks, and what is more, considers other nationalities foreigners no matter how long they have been here, even to the second and third generations. This, even before he has his first papers. This may be due to the fact that he already speaks the language when he lands and is absorbed immediately into the community life of his own people in the city in which he has chosen to settle. Usually he would obtain employment in the building or construction industry as a manual laborer, and as his knowledge increased in his particular line of work, so would his social status increase among his own group.

"Until the beginning of the Depression, the limit of his social conquest was to obtain membership in one of the local middle-class country clubs. The "ultra" social clubs had bans on Jews and Irish Catholics, and in one particular case it was known that an Irish applicant was turned down for no other reason than he was not qualified by birth. This attitude prevailed until the early 1930s, when the fortunes and incomes of the upper crust were sadly depleted and the cost of maintaining such elegant golf courses and clubhouses was more than they could afford. They were faced with the alternative of either admitting a lower social stratum or bankruptcy.

[12] *WPA Federal Writers' Project,* 1939 letter, anonymous.

"They decided the former was the lesser of the two evils, so word was passed that it was possible to join the club even though you were not a direct descendant of one of the first families. The result was that many of the second generation of all nationalties who had become successful as lawyers and doctors hastened to sign up, and their own clubs and groups of friends they had gone through school with were abandoned for the next higher class of society. In some cases, when it became known that membership in the club did not include membership in the social group to which they aspired, they found themselves in somewhat of a dilemma. To retire would acknowledge frustration of their ambitions, but to carry on meant some sacrifice. At this point, some withdrew as graciously as possible.

"In politics, it is evident that more and more Irish are being replaced as professional politicians by other nationalities. The present generation just does not have the desire nor the following that was natural for their forebears. A generation ago, most of the local politics were settled in the respective districts by community leaders of whom the saloon keeper was the ringleader. In most cases, this was an Irishman to whom the neighbors at times looked as a gracious benefactor, because whenever anyone was in trouble due to sickness or misfortune of any kind he was the one they came to, and they were seldom turned away. Of course, at times, he was blamed for most of the trouble that befell the men of the family as a result of their drinking bouts, so at times he was an angel and at other times a devil, depending on the most recent events. But in matters of neighborhood improvement or municipal affairs in their particular districts, it was to him that the people turned. Naturally, when election time came, he was voted into office as their ambassador.

"In religion, the Irish are still the leaders in Catholic Church affairs. While there are probably as many Catholics of other nationalities, the affairs of the city and of the diocese are governed primarily by the Irish. This will probably change in time as Irish of this generation no longer believe in large families and the result of this will be evident in the future as the other nationalities still look upon large families as a blessing. . . ."

## I'M REMINDED OF JOHN ADAMS

In 1975, Dr. O., an Irish-American professional, commented on the future of the Irish community in his own city in Massachusetts, and wondered about the direction the next generation would take.[13]

"There's a lot of talent in the Irish community, but it doesn't necessarily get used in the scholarly sense. There's been a preoccupation with money and status, particularly because it was so hard to come by in the early years. I'm reminded of John Adams' observation that 'I study war and politics in order that my sons may study business and professions in

[13] Fallows, private collection, 1976 interview with Dr. O.

order that their sons may study art and literature'—something like that—and maybe what's happened here is that the Irish are still stuck at stage two. Most Americans are. They're not ready to make this next move, but their children may be. It's taken them a long time to feel it was a worthwhile objective; it never is for the newly rich, is it?

"The next generation will be different, partly I think because of Vatican II and the changes in the Church. Not only are the attitudes of the Irish different toward becoming priests and nuns, but it may have contributed to a disintegration of Irish solidarity. The Church was so much glue that held the family together—the loyalty to the Church, the adherence to the Church's strictures—and that is much looser since Vatican II, I think. There's still a fairly strong Catholic community here, but I feel it's less strong than it would have been fifteen years ago. There are fewer Catholics who go to Mass, and more of the kids who go to non-Catholic colleges seem to drift away from the Church and not drift back. So on the whole it has the effect of making the Irish Americans more like everybody else. There's a sense of loss because of that, because the Irish have not been just like everybody else before."

CHAPTER SEVEN

# The Irish American Family

To understand the structure and impact of the family as it developed in Ireland and America, we must go back to the famine years of the mid-nineteenth century, an experience that not only dramatically altered the family system in Ireland but also led to the creation of the Irish subsociety in America. Robert Kennedy's study of Irish emigration patterns, *The Irish: Emigration, Marriage, and Fertility,* makes clear that, as the final "convincer," the famine was a major "push" factor driving people from rural areas of Ireland; yet he points out that other "push" factors were not insignificant: the narrowing opportunities in industry just prior to the famine, which forced artisans either to emigrate or to return to the land; the squeezing out of unprofitable farms and the eviction of tenant farmers, which left the ten-acre farmers in a relatively worse position and without opportunity to advance themselves; and the loss of hope that any major reform was possible. On the "pull" side were the exaggerated stories of high living standards in America, the word of the California gold discoveries, and the steady flow of passage money from relatives already in America.[1] Even after the famine, when the pressure on rural areas was relieved and farm production began to return to normal, the pattern of emigration continued to draw so many thousand in each decade away from their families that many Irish parents lost nearly all of their children through emigration.

Most of those who left were between the ages of fifteen and thirty-five, for the very young and the elderly had to stay behind. Irish mothers and fathers must have wondered what would be remembered by sons and daughters who left home so young. How would they withstand the dangers and temptations of a new country? How would they raise children of their own who would keep faith with the values that had been passed on from generation to generation in Ireland? The American Wake was the rural family's final ceremony for the departing emigrants—a mixture of mourning for the child who would probably never be seen again and of celebration of a rite of passage, as young adults went out to prove themselves and seek their fortunes in uncharted territory. No other country has lost so high

[1] Robert E. Kennedy, Jr., *The Irish: Emigration, Marriage, and Fertility* (Berkeley: University of California Press, 1973), p. 207.

a proportion of its population to emigration, for today many times more Irish live outside their homeland than in it and there is scarcely an Irish family that does not have part of its lineage in America.

For some of those who crossed the Atlantic, the link between the two family systems has represented a semi-mystical tie with that lineage, whose roots are not only in Ireland but firmly implanted on a particular farm still inhabited by the Irish contingent of the clan. For others the link has been so weak that virtually nothing is known of the past except that an ancestor "came over."[2] Research evidence suggests, however, that traits of an ethnic heritage are often unconsciously transmitted in the intimacy of the family: role expectations for parents and children, religious values, goals to be sought and methods suitable for seeking them, a sense of self-identity, and a place in the scheme of things. Although every family is a unique mini-culture, seldom open to the scrutiny of outsiders and to some extent defying generalization, each such unit is also a conduit for the transmission of cultural values and, insofar as it is supported by an ethnic subsociety, a powerful carrier of ethnic tradition. In this chapter we will compare the changes that occurred in the traditional Irish folk family as it developed on the two sides of the Atlantic and then investigate whether or not significant differences still exist, in attitude or behavior, between those whose socialization has been in Irish American as opposed to Anglo-American families.

## CHANGES IN THE IRISH FOLK FAMILY

Before the famine years, families of southern and western Ireland were traditionally Irish-speaking, Catholic, subsistence farmers whose typical life style involved early marriage, many children, and subdivision of land between brothers upon the withdrawal of the father from farming, or at his death. As we have seen, this pattern had doubtless been instrumental in reducing the Irish to near total reliance on the potato as the only feasible crop and in producing severe overpopulation; but it had also contributed to singularly close family bonds in which the parent generation demanded and received respectful attention, arranged matches for the children to ensure suitable links between families, and provided the model for adult roles that remained unchanged from generation to generation. Under oppression, the extended family, supported by the teachings of the Catholic Church, had been a mainstay against tyranny and disaster. Little education beyond that provided by the parents was needed, and little sought, though in some families an exceptional son trained for the priesthood or an adept daughter became skilled as a midwife. Most, however, remained bound to the land.

[2] Chapter 6, "Self-Portraits of Irish Americans," demonstrates this variation.

In the precarious world of the Irish peasant, the web of cooperation between relatives was well understood, as unspoken debts were incurred and obligations fulfilled to make communal survival possible. And because mankind could not endure without divine help, God's hand was seen in daily events and his design was not to be questioned. "They" were also there, passing by the cottage at night, turning the cream sour and creating mischief for the unwary who failed to observe the courtesies and traditions of the countryside with respect to the "good people" or "fairies."[3] Thus the Irish folk family is steeped in tradition and geared toward clear understanding and ritual observance of ancient, sacred ways. Since there is neither expectation of, nor opportunity for, dramatic change, such changes as do occur are both unanticipated and agonizing in their effects. The famine and its related calamities brought changes of this kind, whose ripple effects are still being felt.

### Creation of the National Schools

Although Ireland had been under English rule for 700 years, formal education had been severely limited by the British. For this reason, many isolated farm families still spoke Irish until after the famine years, when the Irish-speaking stock was split into two branches.[4] One branch learned to speak English in the National Schools, which were first established in Ireland by the British government in 1831, and the other branch learned to speak American on the other side of the Atlantic. Despite some initial resentment at having to learn the language of their oppressors, by 1875 the Irish had become a highly literate population who could communicate with the majority of their countrymen on both sides of the Atlantic. Children did not always attend school regularly because of the distances involved, the doubt about how much use an education would be, the need to work on the farms, and the unavailability of National Schools in some areas, but increasingly the younger generations acquired familiarity with English which made contact with a wider social world possible.

Letters and money arriving from America revealed the gap between the standard of living of recent emigrants and those who had remained at home, thus raising the aspirations of young Irish men and women. Not only were living conditions in the mother country improved by the 260 million dollars in "America money" that was sent back between 1848 and 1900, but this money also paid for three-fourths of the emigration from Ireland to America.[5] Knowing that they would be received by relatives who spoke a common language was a strong incentive to emigrate. Through a common

[3] For a discussion of the "good people" or fairies in Irish folk belief, see Conrad Arensberg, *The Irish Countryman* (Garden City: The Natural History Press, 1968), Ch. 6.
[4] Conor Cruise O'Brien, *States of Ireland* (New York: Arno Press, 1969), pp. 44–45.
[5] Kennedy, *The Irish,* p. 23.

language, too, those who stayed home were encouraged to rebel by those who had left but who had not forgotten why they had been forced to leave. When families are separated not only by an ocean, but also by a language, as has happened with the majority of non-English-speaking immigrant groups, the ties weaken over generations and eventually dissolve. Because all but the most remote and isolated families in Ireland became familiar with English, however, this never happened for the Irish.

### The End of Multiple Inheritance

The Irish family changed in still another profound way because of the famine years. Where formerly a family farm would be split up among the sons and all of them would remain on the land, after the famine years it became necessary to limit inheritance to just one son who would take over the farm while the rest stayed on as unmarried and unpaid helpers, emigrated to America or elsewhere, or were fortunate enough to have apprenticeships or landed marriages arranged for them. The "stem family system," in which only one child inherits control over family property, is, in Kennedy's view, "the essential social institution which motivated and permitted individuals to remain permanently single, or to marry at a relatively late age" if they remained in Ireland rather than emigrating.[6] In family life, the husband-wife and father-son relationships hardened and took on a more strained character as the realities of single inheritance were borne in on family members. Since marriage itself was largely dependent on inheritance of land, and since it normally could not occur until the father was willing to hand over control of the farm to his son, many males could not marry at all, and those who did so married late. As a result, Ireland became unique in demographic studies, as it consistently decreased in population from 1841 to 1961.[7] The proportion postponing marriage or remaining permanently single was higher than in any other European nation, yet among those who did marry the birth rate was Europe's highest.

In spite of the combined social and religious supports that bolstered the status of the single person—that is, he was respected as normal rather than regarded as deviant, and he profited from the increased emphasis on sexual Puritanism which entered Irish Catholicism at about this time—it is not hard to visualize the strain on families as sons reached marriageable age. If the young men could not marry, neither, of course, could the young women. Thus, for both men and women, the future for all but a small portion of their original cohorts held the likelihood of emigration, postponement of marriage until their thirties or later, or permanent celibacy. Those who decided upon emigration had sized up their economic, social, and matrimonial chances as better in another country, and their numbers in-

[6] *Ibid.,* p. 13.
[7] *Ibid.,* p. 1.

cluded a high proportion of girls who would, in fact, find the husbands in America that they were unlikely to find in Ireland. For this reason, the American Irish commonly trace their families back to marriages performed after the young immigrants had arrived in this country and somewhat established themselves.

### The Consequences of Male Dominance

For those men who remained in Ireland, the change in family structure resulting from the single inheritance was instrumental in reinforcing the already existing male institution of the bachelor group. The strong emphases on sexual chastity and celibacy promoted segregation of the sexes which resulted in intensive male grouping. Since the father-son relationship tended to be strained by the requirements of the single inheritance, bachelor groups were frequently led by a married man who assumed an avuncular relationship with the young bachelors, and who passed on the bachelor group ideals of adventure, instinctive action, hard drinking, and freedom from responsibility.

Richard Stivers, who has analyzed the role of the bachelor group ethic in continuing the tradition of hard drinking as a symbol of machismo in Ireland and America between 1840 and 1940, has noted the cohesiveness of the stable bachelor group in Ireland. Comparing the bachelor group to the highly anomic conditions under which men gathered in all-male groupings in America, he concludes that the Irish institution was a major contributor to less pathological drinking behavior.[8] Although drinking was by no means the only activity of the bachelor group in Ireland, it was usually in this group's company that the young man took his first formal drink in a public house, and it was in line with the group's norms for drinking behavior that he learned the use and abuse of alcohol. However, it was also in the bachelor group that he learned something of his place in society.

Conrad Arensberg, describing the countryman's ways in the remote southwestern part of Ireland as late as the 1930s, tells of the sociable evening gatherings of the old men's groups around a cottage fire where they discussed the crops, pondered the social and political needs of the community, and came to sober judgments about their world.[9] By contrast, the young men's groups passed the time with less sense of purpose, and with the uncomfortable recognition that they were years removed from status and prestige in the community. In time, they too might join the dignified group of old men who were respected family heads, but it was also quite within the realm of possibility that they would remain perpetual "boys" in the

[8] Richard Stivers, "The Bachelor Group Ethic and Irish Drinking," Unpublished Doctoral Dissertation, Southern Illinois University, 1971.

[9] Arensberg, *The Irish Countryman,* Ch. 4.

eyes of the community. A bachelor group, then, was not necessarily composed of dashing young fellows. It might be composed instead of those who were lacking in status, or unmarried, or both.

But if dominance by older males put many of the young men in an unenviable position, dominance by men of any age put women in an even less enviable one. Women customarily walked behind their husbands, even if they were going somewhere together, ate after the men had finished, were expected to help with the men's work in addition to doing their own (a practice the men were not obliged to reciprocate), and were expected to give preferential treatment to the sons in the family. In addition, men were not accountable for the income from the sale of animals or cash crops, and might use these as they saw fit, even if it meant that the money was irresponsibly squandered in drinking and gambling. "There was the chance," Kennedy points out, "that the wife and children would be supported by leftovers, with the sons getting the largest share."[10] Both high female mortality and the emigration of young farm girls to Irish urban areas and to the United States are closely linked to the extreme male dominance that has persisted into the twentieth century in Ireland, as Kennedy's analysis amply demonstrates.

## The Bachelor Husband

Both male dominance and the bachelor group ethic persist as an influence on Irish family life even in the 1970s, according to Donald Connery, whose discussion of contemporary Irish marriage includes a description of the "married bachelor."[11] The prototype of the married bachelor is the male who has become so accustomed to his freedom and the lack of responsibility of bachelor group activities that he continues them even after marriage. A marriage counselor quoted by Connery describes the married bachelor's principal aim, when he does marry, as one of making sure that his marriage will interfere as little as possible with his established routine of activities with male friends—activities having little to do with sex.

> In the intimate side of marriage he behaves as if he were slightly ashamed of having deserted his male friends and his bachelorhood. . . . A rapid sex routine is effected, as if his wife is some stray creature with whom he is sinning and hopes he may never see again. . . . Though many Irish wives are preconditioned to such behavior, having seen its like in their own fathers and uncles, they resent it deeply. But as they turn from their husbands to lavish their attention on their sons, and then, in later years, strive to "protect" the sons from scheming girls wishing to marry them, they carry on the vicious circle of maternal possessiveness and male selfishness.[12]

[10] Kennedy, *The Irish,* p. 53.
[11] Donald S. Connery, *The Irish* (New York: Simon and Schuster, 1970), Ch. 6.
[12] *Ibid.,* p. 200.

To anyone who knows the Irish scene, Connery insists, all of this is familiar, yet there is little hard sociological evidence on the subject, since of course sociologists are not ordinarily privy to the intimate affairs that are discussed with marriage counselors, nor are those who approach marriage counselors for advice necessarily typical. Nevertheless, the undisputed pattern of male dominance, combined with the persistence of the bachelor group ethic and its intrusion upon married life for over a century, suggest that for those who remained in Ireland the ideal pattern of young marriage and large families, thwarted as it was by economic conditions, put an intense strain on family life.

Perhaps the strain would have been far more intense, were it not for the fact that thousands of young Irish who were unwilling to wait for marriage in Ireland—and anxious to leave the protective custody of parents—were siphoned off through emigration to America. Kennedy concludes that the high percentage of women emigrants can also be attributed to two other factors: the ease with which English-speaking young women were able to find jobs as domestics in America and the fact that, in spite of the extreme male dominance in Ireland, women were as free to emigrate from rural Ireland as were young men. By the 1870s, moreover, while women were gaining in social status in America, the position of young single women in Ireland was actually growing worse.[13] There were multiple reasons for both young men and women to emigrate, then, including the lack of prospects for landless young men, the inability of many to marry in Ireland, the chance for women to emancipate themselves from the severe male dominance in their families, and finally the chance to be where the "pool of eligibles" was.

## THE PATTERN FOR IRISH AMERICAN FAMILIES

There was excitement attached to going to America, as well as hope for social and economic improvement. Since communication across the Atlantic was continuous, it was not difficult to find a relative to sponsor the trip. For generations, each emigrant who went to America had a fixed responsibility to send back money and to pay the passage for a brother or sister who would follow. "Sending for a greenhorn" became an established practice which carried with it the additional responsibility in this country of finding a job for the newcomer and for as many other relatives and neighbors from Ireland as possible. The Irish neighborhood was the social context for the meeting and pairing off of the young immigrants. The Irish woman who told in the previous chapter about being the fourth in her family to emigrate, of joining a sister who married soon after, of meeting her

[13] Kennedy, *The Irish,* p. 84.

own future husband at one of many Irish social affairs, and of being wed only eight years after arriving in America, was telling a success story. She fulfilled that part of the ideal pattern for the rural Irish Catholic family that came to be emphasized in America: young marriage and many children. The other elements of that pattern were, out of necessity, emphasized in Ireland: deference for parents, respectful waiting for inheritance of land before assuming adult responsibilities, or staying on as unpaid, unmarried contributors on the family farm.

### Mate Selection and Endogamy

While the early Irish Catholics were desperately poor by American standards, they were relatively prosperous by comparison with many of those who had remained in Ireland. They had accepted the view that the future was wide open and that one's children might achieve anything. Even with widening horizons in their adopted country, there were, of course, those who remained single because the years of famine had inspired extreme caution, or because they were concentrating on personal upward mobility, or because their own needs could be fulfilled within the structure of an expanding Catholic Church in America. The norm, however, was to find a mate and to raise a devout Catholic family. The majority of the Irish looked to their own subsociety to accomplish these goals.

The social pressures involved in mate selection and the degree of endogamy within the Irish Catholic group that have been touched on in previous chapters suggest several norms that had developed for the establishment of families:

1. Marriage within the Irish Catholic community was considered preferable, especially in the early years, and was usually possible because of the tendency to group in Irish settlements where the young could meet each other.

2. Older-generation Irish Americans, as settled and respected members of an established community, had higher prestige than Irish-born newcomers.

3. Marriage with non-Irish Catholics was a permissible alternative to marriage within the Irish community, but followed a preference hierarchy in which the earlier-arriving Catholics—English or German—were considered more suitable than the later-arriving Catholics of the "new immigration."

4. By the third generation, there was some tendency for the socially aspiring to marry Protestants, or to convert to Protestantism, although this was disapproved.

In stable communities, intermarriage between families is one of the clearest indications of social acceptance and status equality. However, for the young Irish men and women who had left their families behind, the forming of alliances focused more on achieved than on ascribed status. Counterbalancing this tendency to select a mate based on personal achievements and prospects were the traditional social pressures of settled ethnic neighborhoods and the teaching of the Catholic Church. These worked hand in hand. Birmingham has pointed out that in the Irish view of Catholicism:

> To be an Irish Catholic . . . was in itself a mark of social and religious superiority. Second in importance to the Irish Catholic came the German Catholic, and after the Germans came the English. . . . Much further down the ladder came the French, Italian, Belgian, Spanish, Portuguese, and all the other kinds of Catholics—simply because the Catholics of these countries were not as conscientious about their religion.[14]

Since Catholic immigrants of various ethnic groups were socially isolated from each other in many communities—not only because of the pattern of ethnic settlement but also because the Catholic Church provided for "national parishes" where ethnic congregations worshiped in their own language under the leadership of compatriot priests—the young Irish might simply never meet those Catholics of other nationality groups. In some New England communities, even at mid-twentieth century, the pattern has persisted whereby Irish, German, and French-Canadian descendants of earlier immigrants still attend separate parochial schools and separate parish churches. In earlier years, the pattern was even more pronounced.

Bessie Wessel's study of ethnic intermarriage patterns in Woonsocket, Rhode Island, in 1931, throws some light on ways in which approved norms for marriage were altered by circumstances peculiar to a given community. In an ethnic study of nearly 5,000 parents of school-age children, Wessel found that 62 percent of all Irish parents who had married in the United States, cutting across all generations, had married within their own ethnic group; when the responses were limited to first-generation parents, the percent marrying endogamously was 78. Among the men of all generations who had married here, 66 percent had married within the Irish community, with a preference for French Canadian women and those of mixed Irish and other ethnic heritage when they married outside it. Among the women, 58 percent had married endogamously, with a clear preference for American-born French Canadian men, followed by British, and finally men of mixed descent when they married outside their own group.[15]

Clearly, the Irish of Woonsocket who had married in the first quarter of this century had not followed the pattern of socio-religious preference sketched by Birmingham for exogamous marriages. The explanation lies in

[14] Stephen Birmingham, *Real Lace: America's Irish Rich* (New York: Harper & Row, 1973), p. 223.

[15] Bessie Bloom Wessel, *An Ethnic Survey of Woonsocket, Rhode Island* (Chicago: University of Chicago Press, 1931), pp. 135–39.

the fact that there were almost no Germans in Woonsocket, and fewer English than Irish (certainly *far* fewer who would also be Catholic), but that there were three times as many French Canadians as Irish. The law of propinquity in mate selection was certainly a factor. Meeting is an obvious prerequisite to marrying, unless the marriage is an arranged one, and the French Canadians were the most numerous Catholic ethnic group with whom the single Irish might have come in contact. If they were also regarded as of lower socio-religious prestige, this was balanced by choosing an American-born French Canadian who was one step up in terms of generational status.

Later studies of ethnic endogamy among the Irish include Ruby Jo Reeves Kennedy's analysis of marriage patterns in New Haven between 1897 and 1950, which showed that the endogamous marriage rate for people of Irish descent in that city had dropped to 50 percent by mid-century, but that while national origin barriers in marriage had tended to break down, there was a continued pattern for Catholics to marry within their own religious "pool." (Since Protestants and Jews were following the same pattern of marriage within their own "pools," she labeled this the "triple melting pot" effect.)[16]

More recently still, Harold Abramson's analysis of the degree of endogamy among Irish Catholics (see the discussion in Chapter 5) found that among males aged 23 to 57, 43 percent had married within their own Irish American group compared with 65 percent of the previous generation.[17] Although we cannot generalize about the broader patterns for Irish Americans as a whole from community studies, the studies of Woonsocket and New Haven parallel the trend toward increased exogamy that is reflected in the national study. Moreover, the national study confirms the ethnic preferences noted by Birmingham when exogamous marriages do occur. In the parental generation, in Abramson's study, the order of preference was for German first, English second, and French Canadian third. In the respondent's generation the same pattern prevailed except for the substitution of Italians for French Canadians.[18]

In a later analysis of the same data used by Abramson, Richard D. Alba has further refined the concept of an endogamous marriage by discounting from this data base any marriage that was a product of earlier intermarriages with other ethnic groups.[19] Classifying marriages as

[16] Ruby Jo Reeves Kennedy, "Single or Triple Melting-Pot? Intermarriage in New Haven, 1870–1950," *American Journal of Sociology,* 58, No. 1 (July 1952), 56.

[17] Harold Abramson, *Ethnic Diversity in Catholic America* (New York: John Wiley and Sons, 1973), p. 53. The possibility emerges that Irish American males are somewhat more likely to marry endogamously than are females, as was true in the Woonsocket study in 1931. I am not aware of any data at the national level that would confirm this, however.

[18] *Ibid.,* p. 58

[19] Richard D. Alba, "Social Assimilation Among American Catholic National-Origin Groups," *American Sociological Review,* 41 (December 1976), 1030–46.

endogamous only if there is pure Irish ancestry through the grandparents' generation on both sides, Alba finds that only 31 percent of Irish Catholic marriages are endogamous, and that 61 percent of the Irish in the sample were themselves of mixed ancestry. Alba found that the degree of mixed ancestry increased by generation from 28 percent in the first to 68 percent in the fourth or later generation, and concluded that with such an ethnically mixed kinship network there is little to support the view of a structurally separate Irish Catholic subsociety. He was careful to point out, however, that the separation from an ethnically enclosed Irish community represented by this mixed kinship network did not necessarily imply integration into a majority group; rather it implied only that the social network would include those of other ethnic backgrounds.

The interpretation we make of these figures for endogamy and for mixed ethnic background will depend on our assumptions about the persistence of ethnic subsocieties. If we start with the assimilationist assumption that after several generations in this country any tendency to marry endogamously will have evaporated (except for clearly stigmatized groups) and that social class will have replaced ethnicity as the prime factor in mate selection, then the fact that 30 to 40 percent of Irish Americans still choose mates from among those of pure Irish ancestry comes as something of a surprise. If, on the other hand, we assume that ethnic preferences persist into an indefinite future—or at least so long as remnants of an ethnic subsociety remain to support them—then a mere 30 to 40 percent of endogamous marriages may seem low. Given the fact that Irish Catholics today comprise only 18 percent of American Catholics, it would seem quite unlikely that so high a percentage would marry within their own ethnic group by chance. When we add to these inferences the facts that close to 70 percent of Irish Americans are of the third or later generation and that the majority have long since moved from their self-enclosed ethnic neighborhoods, it becomes apparent that there continue to be clear preferences for mate selection. It is equally apparent, however, from Alba's study that the majority (61 percent) of Irish Americans are of mixed ethnic backgrounds.

## THE PERSISTENCE OF ETHNIC TRAITS

Most American Irish, whether of pure or mixed ancestry, are far removed in time and space from the rural folk families their ancestors left. If any ethnic traits remain to distinguish them from Americans of other ethnic backgrounds, they are not immediately apparent. Daniel P. Moynihan has observed that it is "when the immigrants first arrive that everyone is aware of them. By the time the problems are less severe, or have become largely personal, local color has been dissipated in the flush of Americanization."[20] When we turn to a discussion of ethnic traits among the American Irish, it is apparent that little of the "local color"—the characteristic brogue, wit, or song—remains specifically Irish today. Does this merging into the general American culture mean that the Irish have no distinctive characteristics remaining? William Shannon points out that while the Irish arrived with no distinctive cuisine, language, culture, or body of national customs, what they share is "a pair of intangibles: an outlook on life formed by centuries of defeat, subjugation and alien occupation of their native country and a Catholic religion darkened by the same past."[21]

Ethnic traits, then, can be intangibles which are transmitted through the socialization of children in the privacy of family life—even after all conscious awareness of them has been lost. If such traits remain, they could be expected to reflect only some aspects of the original culture, whereas other aspects would be dropped, replaced, or modified. The result would be an interpretation of the world and of appropriate social roles that would duplicate neither the world view of the host society nor that of the country of origin. Patently, each of us lives in a different private reality. Yet in his study of the reactions to pain among men from four different ethnic backgrounds, Mark Zborowski concludes that early socialization experiences within a given ethnic group are similar enough to be able to predicate typical reactions for various ethnic groups to specific situations.[22] It is in these intangible ways that an ethnic group may retain its distinctive approach to life, without even being aware of it. While the persistence of ethnic traits for the Irish could be expected to vary by social class, length of time in America, extent of intermarriage, and a host of other variables, the available data do not permit such an in-depth analysis. Nonetheless, National Opinion Research Center (NORC) studies do throw light on two areas in which comparisons can be made: selected attitudes and behavior of Irish Catholics and the structure of the Irish Catholic family.

## Selected Attitudes and Behavior of Irish Catholics

In a study based on representative samples of Irish and Anglo-Americans, Andrew Greeley and William McCready have attempted to define which, if any, characteristics of Irish Americans in the 1960s could be predicted on the basis of known culture traits of the rural Catholic Irish.[23] They based

[20] Nathan Glazer and Daniel P. Moynihan, *Beyond the Melting Pot* (Cambridge: MIT Press, 1970), p. 22.

[21] William Shannon, "The Lasting Hurrah," *The New York Times Magazine,* March 14, 1976, p. 75.

[22] Mark Zborowski, *People in Pain* (San Francisco: Jossey-Bass, 1969), Ch. 1.

[23] Andrew M. Greeley and William C. McCready, "The Transmission of Cultural Heritages: The Case of the Irish and Italians," in Nathan Glazer and Daniel P. Moynihan, *Ethnicity: Theory and Experience* (Cambridge: Harvard University Press, 1975), pp. 209–35.

their research on anthropological studies of the folk family in the extreme west of Ireland (which, despite the fact that several generations had elapsed between the famine years and the time the studies were made, they felt had retained much of the same structure and value system). On this basis, then, they proposed twenty-five hypotheses covering expected differences between Irish Americans in the 1960s and their Anglo-American counterparts. Of their original twenty-five hypotheses, seven—slightly less than one-third—were confirmed at the statistically significant level. The tragedy of a hypothesis shot down by a fact is commonplace in scientific research, but what is intriguing is that roughly 30 percent of the hypotheses *were* borne out by the data, showing that persistent differences do carry over into the third and later generations. Even more significant is the fact that these differences could have been predicted from a folk family that had itself changed from the time of the famine. That the data fail to support other hypotheses at a statistically significant level, or actually run counter to the hypotheses, is not surprising when we consider that the Irish have adapted to a totally different culture and an urban way of life.

In the following summary of Greeley and McCready's findings, the characteristics that ran counter to the direction of their hypotheses are italicized. By focusing on the italicized characteristics only, one can see ways in which the Irish, in the process of adapting to American life, have not only learned to think and behave like their Anglo-American hosts but in some ways have actually overconformed. Those characteristics that are not italicized were the ones that confirmed the original hypotheses based on predictions from the culture of the Irish folk society. Those so labeled, at the end, showed no significant differences between Irish and Anglo-Americans.

In a national sample of Anglo-American Protestant males and Irish American Catholic males, the Irish were more fatalistic, *less authoritarian, less anxious,* and *more trusting* than Anglo-Americans. In political behavior, the Irish were more likely to vote, more likely to campaign, and *more respectful of the political process.* In a representative sample of female college graduates, Irish American women differed in their attitudes toward the family in that they were more likely than their Anglo-American counterparts to view the wife-mother role as the dominant one in marriage, to view the mother's working as detrimental to her children, and to see the woman as a helpmate to her husband. They were *less likely to stress security as important, or to stress the importance of keeping up family contacts or relationships with parents or in-laws,* or to feel that a daughter's independence was important. They were *less likely to report tense relationships with their mothers,* but more likely to report such relationships with their fathers. Areas in which differences were predicted but in which none emerged as significant included the following: drinking behavior, the likelihood of having drinking problems, degree of sexual restrictiveness for males, and degree of sexual restrictiveness for females.

When the authors held constant the regional and educational differences between Irish and Anglo-Americans for one of the "harder" sets of variables being measured—political behavior—the differences remained significant. Nor can the mere fact of Catholic versus Protestant upbringing be identified as the crucial factor accounting for the differences, since, in the same study, Italians (also Catholics) displayed markedly different characteristics from the Irish. What this suggests is that there are still characteristic approaches to life, even for an ethnic group which is overwhelmingly in the third or later generation of life in America, and that these show no signs of abating. With the clarity of hindsight, we can rationalize the changes that have occurred, and that were not predictable on the basis of the folk culture of rural Ireland. In response to centuries of subjugation and defeat, male authoritarianism, anxiety, lack of trust, lack of respect for the political process, and emphasis on security were normal, not paranoid, reactions. In response to the precarious existence of the folk family, emphasis on family ties—yet resentment of the father's authority—were also quite human responses. But under wholly new conditions in America, those immigrants whose lives were more hopeful may have perceived these same responses as unnecessary or even un-American. On the other hand, those differences which were sensed as having high survival value—for instance, voting, the wife-mother role, or fatalism—would have been too important to ignore in the socialization of children, and would have been retained. The modification of culture is always a selective process.

## Family Structure of Irish Catholics

In terms of family structure, the SuperNORC composite sample of close to 18,000 Americans (see Chapter 5, pp. 65–66) shows that Irish Catholics are less likely than British Protestants (or any other Protestant group) to marry before the age of twenty-one, less likely to become divorced, less likely to approve of the wife's working, and more likely to have three or more children. (The mean for Irish families is 2.6 as against the British Protestant mean of 2.1 and the national mean of 2.4) There is some evidence that attitudes of Catholics, including Irish, are changing toward family planning, as the rhythm method is being replaced by use of the pill, which has led Greeley to conclude that Protestant-Catholic family sizes of the future may be quite similar.[24]

While attitudes toward legal abortion show that a majority of Irish Catholics in metropolitan areas of the North support the legal availability of abortion for those who wish to use it—especially in cases of rape, a threat

[24] Andrew M. Greeley, *The American Catholic: A Social Portrait* (New York: Basic Books, Inc., 1977), pp. 188–89. Chapter 10 in *The American Catholic,* which deals with family structure, brings together relevant data from the SuperNORC composite sample, some parts of which were also analyzed in Greeley's *Ethnicity, Denomination, and Inequality.*

to the mother's life, or the likelihood of birth defects—their support runs well below that of British Protestants under the same conditions. Irish Catholics are far less sympathetic toward other reasons for abortion, for example, as a form of birth control to avoid having more children, because of poverty, or because the woman does not want to marry. These attitudes parallel those of other Catholic and Protestant groups, though the degree of disapproval is greater than among Protestants.[25]

When we leave the family characteristics that are directly influenced by Catholic teaching and moral stance to consider the interpersonal dynamics of family life, the Irish emerge as having somewhat contradictory characteristics. In data collected for the National Institute of Mental Health by NORC in the 1960s, the Irish ranked first among eight ethnic groups in time spent with the children and in amount of hugging and kissing of children, but also first in amount of child scolding. In time spent with their spouses, the Irish ranked third—below Italian and Slavic Catholics, but well above British Protestants who ranked seventh. The picture that emerges is of an affectionate family in which time and attention are lavished on children, but in which more than the normal amount of attention takes the form of scolding.[26]

The Irish American family gives every evidence of having what Greeley refers to as a "rebellious" combination of a high degree of central power or control, along with a low degree of support in family relationships. Greeley comments:

> The Irish family, apparently very active in its relationships and both centralized and unsupportive, produces a personality that seems a bundle of contradictions—low on authoritarianism and moralism, high on fatalism and trust, and also high on both inner- and outer-direction. Catholic families, in other words, are different, and different personalities seem to develop from these families. The melting pot has not burned away all the differences in expectations and values that remain after immigration, but we have only the dimmest perception of how these differing values, styles, and personalities are transmitted.[27]

There seems little doubt that subtle differences do persist, partly as a product of a common ethnic history and experience which no longer receive explicit attention but which are built into the family structure and passed on virtually unconsciously. Yet, where family characteristics are concerned, social class may be of more significance than ethnic heritage. Except in ethnic neighborhoods, child raising, husband-wife relationships, power distribution, and moral questions tend to become at least superficially homogenized by a total community experience of work, school,

[25] *Ibid.,* p. 246.
[26] *Ibid.,* p. 195.
[27] *Ibid.,* pp. 202–3.

and free-time activities. Below this superficial level undoubtedly lie all the variations which ethnicity has contributed to the American pattern; yet it seems doubtful that these intergroup variations are any greater than those existing *within* each group.

Parents who urge their children to "marry someone like yourself" are at least partially aware of the possible strain that can result when unconscious ethnic differences emerge under stress in family interaction, and they may be expressing more than ethnic or social class defensiveness in trying to protect their children from such stresses. To judge from the fact that the majority of Irish marriages are taking place with those of other ethnic backgrounds, it would seem that many younger people are willing to disregard the ethnic, if not the social class, implications of such advice. Since the Irish have an unusually low divorce rate—seven percent[28]—it may be that the differences are not as problematic as they once might have appeared to be. In most important respects, it would appear, the Irish family has become simply an American family.

[28] *Ibid.,* p. 188.

CHAPTER EIGHT

# The Irish in Politics

What individuals or groups get out of politics normally depends on how much they participate in political life. Those Irish Catholics who arrived in a singularly concentrated wave in the mid-1800s, and who congregated in urban areas where the power of their votes could be effectively mobilized, burst on the American political scene with every intention not only of participating in political life but of getting something out of it as well. Having been excluded from effective access to political power in Ireland and having known the frustrations of the exploited, they were ready to make up for past deprivations and to make their influence felt as speedily as possible. In some ways, they were as politically sophisticated as they were culturally and economically unsophisticated. From the campaigns of Daniel O'Connell, who had led the movement for Catholic emancipation and repeal of the Act of Union in Ireland during the 1820s through the 1840s, many had already learned the skills of competition within the Anglo-Saxon political system, the art of confrontation politics, and the uses of compromise. They were soon joined in America by leaders from the abortive revolution of the Young Irelanders, who sought to mobilize Irish strength in America through the uniting issue of a free Ireland. And they had their own desperate need for jobs and for security in a strange and hostile urban environment, where local political power could work to their immediate advantage.[1]

The descent of the famine Irish on America also coincided with the development of a new American political style which would respond to ethnic needs through the politics of accommodation. With Andrew Jackson's presidency in the 1830s, the Democrats emerged as an enduring political party that would become the focus for Irish loyalties, and the era of the modern political "boss" was launched in burgeoning American cities. Thus, the Irish of the mid-1800s were the first to arrive in sufficient numbers and with sufficient political awareness to recognize that if they hoped

[1] Works dealing with Irish-American nationalism and Irish political life in America include the following, on which this chapter draws: Thomas N. Brown, *Irish-American Nationalism* (New York: J. B. Lippincott Co., 1966); Nathan Glazer and Daniel P. Moynihan, *Beyond the Melting Pot* (Cambridge: MIT Press, 1970); Edgar Litt, *Beyond Pluralism: Ethnic Politics in America* (Glencoe, Ill.: Scott, Foresman and Co., 1970); Joseph P. O'Grady, *How the Irish Became Americans* (New York: Twayne Publishers, Inc., 1973); and William Shannon, *The American Irish* (New York: Macmillan, 1963).

to achieve either freedom for their homeland or security and influence in America they would do well to begin by winning the political power to make the rest possible. And the means to win that power was at hand.

Grass-roots political activity began first in the immigrant slums of every city where the Irish Catholics settled. Building upon a perception of a common fate which transcended their Irish village and county identities, they began to weave their transplanted folk values into a political style and structure that came to be identified as characteristically Irish. The politician was a pivotal figure in the complex pattern of loyalties that marked the Irish neighborhoods—a realist who was less concerned with abstract notions of public service and good government than with the practical concerns of keeping himself in office by building up a patronage system that would bind politician and constituent together in a web of mutual obligation and loyalty. Politics was a career open to the self-made man as were few others, and along with the priesthood and union leadership it became one of the most heavily traveled roads to success for the Irish. So began the hegemony of the Irish in urban ethnic politics—a hegemony that would endure into this century and that would set patterns for other ethnic groups as they too attempted to acquire the leverage to affect political decisions and reap political rewards.

Although its effects are visible, power is difficult to measure, for those who already have it wield it inconspicuously and with assurance, whereas those who are without it often seem heavy-handed and violent in achieving it, as did the Irish in those early years. Their enthusiasm for political roles, combined with their pragmatic view of politics as a system for the distribution of power rather than as an exercise in democratic principles, won them few friends among the Yankees whose power was on the wane. But the early acquisition of political power made possible relief for the destitute, protection from gross exploitation, occupational opportunity through patronage jobs, and forms of both social and personal power at a time when they were not available by any other means.

In the late 1850s, the Irish were influencing American political affairs primarily at the neighborhood and local level; by the 1860s the Irish were in control of Tammany Hall in New York; by the 1870s they were in control of the Democratic party machine in Brooklyn, and were beginning to win seats in Congress. By the 1890s, Philadelphia, Buffalo, Chicago, St. Louis, San Francisco, and Boston were all dominated by the Irish. Yet at the turn of the century Irish politicians, whose strength had previously depended on the "Irish vote" and who had only been able to move beyond the local level when unique issues or voting patterns gave special significance to their local areas, began to win important appointments and political victories solely on their personal merits. By the 1930s the era of the big-city Irish political machine was in decline, and the Irish style in politics was in transition to a more urbane and less parochial approach. By the

1940s, New York was no longer a city politically controlled by the Irish, and even in other cities where urban Democratic councils were still dominated by the Irish, politicians of other ethnic backgrounds were moving up from the lower ranks to replace them. It was time, in the 1950s, for the Irish to try again for a dramatic bid for the highest political office of all and to help put an Irish Catholic in the presidency. By the time John F. Kennedy moved to the White House, Robert Frost's inaugural admonition to "be more Irish than Harvard" told the American Irish that not only their power but their Irishness had been symbolically legitimized. Such a feat set a precedent that will hold for all time.

The lure of politics, and the interweaving of power, prestige, and wealth in the aspirations of the Irish Catholics in America, have been themes throughout earlier chapters. Frequent reference has been made to the big-city political machines which were developed, dominated, and given their distinctive stamp by the Irish, to the political pressure brought to bear on events in Ireland, and to the anti-Catholic sentiment that made political success at the national level so hard to achieve and so long in coming. In the pages that follow, each of these aspects of political behavior will be discussed more systematically to see what remains today of the differences in style, attitude, and policy which they represented.

## THE RISE AND DECLINE OF THE BIG-CITY POLITICAL MACHINE

The Irish became politically involved in America as soon as—and sometimes before—they were registered voters, and long before they had the social status attributes that normally go with active political participation. The investment in politics involved time, effort, and money, but if the risks were great the rewards were also great. Normally it made a real difference who was elected to office at the local level, because the job, the protection, and the security were gone if one's candidate lost. Relatively few Americans today see political choice in such immediate and personal terms as did the Irish in their early years in America.

Machine politics evolved as an urban phenomenon in the last half of the nineteenth century to provide a stable institutional pattern at a time when cities themselves were in a state of flux and when American political standards were at a low ebb. In Chicago, Detroit, Boston, New York, Philadelphia—wherever uprooted people were cut off from the informal social supports on which rural society had depended to take care of social welfare in the 1800s—the effects of unemployment, a bad winter, or an epidemic were disastrous. Private philanthropies were strained and incapable of handling the numbers of destitute, and the national supports on which we depend today had not been visualized. No one stood between the urban worker and disaster, particularly if he was not only new to the city but also new to the country. The "boss" and his political machine filled this void.

The rationale behind the urban political machine which the Irish were to dominate for so many decades is described by Edgar Litt in *Ethnic Politics in America:*

> It met three basic needs of ethnic members, providing social welfare, political privileges, and alternative channels for social mobility. . . . In most American cities, the political machine began with the Irish politician, and the contest for immigrant votes had the effects of breaking down social separation of immigrant communities and making their members active political participants. In return, political participation and social achievement fostered recognition within the community's economic and social spheres. The long-term advantage of ethnicizing political organizations, such as party machines, was that it provided a ready base of local support and a criterion for distributing political benefits. Ethnic consciousness became an integral aspect of party loyalty and organization. . . . [2]

The form that machine governments developed in urban areas was an adaptation of Irish rural custom to the demands of city life, through the privileges of the American political system. "The ancient world of folkways and the modern world of contracts came suddenly together," as Daniel P. Moynihan has described it, with the result that machine politics took on the same stable, hierarchical relationships that were familiar from the rural village "in which almost everyone had a role to play, under the surveillance of a stern oligarchy of elders, and in which, on the whole, a person's position was likely to improve with time."[3]

Not only did the structural form of urban machines parallel the form of stable hierarchical village life, but the ideologies that supported the goals of the machines also drew from Irish experiences. In the struggle for freedom in their homeland, the Irish had learned the importance of defending the rights of the individual, of accepting compromise as better than no gain at all, and of manipulating the balance of power to achieve their ends. They had been politically Anglicized to the extent that they could operate within a constitutional governmental framework through compromise and pressure to gain concessions, but at the same time they brought a distinctly Catholic view of man's imperfections that set them apart from the Anglo-American view of the perfectability of man and the belief in social progress. Thus, in the actual setting of urban life, Irish politicians did not adopt the laissez faire creed of the Anglo-American leaders, but instead undertook to provide help for the needy through the largess of the machine. The Irish political view of social justice was pragmatic and communal rather than ideological and individualistic. Man and society were far from perfect, but one simply did what could be done for those whose background and loyalty

[2] Litt, *Ethnic Politics in America,* p. 45.
[3] Glazer and Moynihan, *Beyond the Melting Pot,* p. 226.

marked them as part of one's social world and deserving of protection. The machine was the instrument through which a simple, though often inefficient, form of social welfare was administered.

The narrow limits of the ethnic neighborhoods were ideally suited to the development of machine politics, for no machine was stronger than the precinct organization that brought out the vote. At the lowest level of organization, the precinct captain and his assistants were responsible for distributing jobs and favors so as to carry his precinct's votes for the machine candidates. The strength of the machine lay in a genuine loyalty that developed between machine workers and voters, many of whom did not consider their votes of crucial importance and who did not see why they shouldn't do a simple favor for a friend. The service and favors provided by the precinct captains or by the more powerful ward bosses above them in the hierarchy, who might have several hundred patronage jobs to distribute, might be no more than the voter was entitled to as a taxpayer, but both gave a feeling of a personal and direct link with a complex bureaucratic government where the average citizen might become lost and helpless. The machine offered predictability and power in a world where the ethnic voter felt himself individually powerless.

For the Irish, who almost from the beginning equated the Republican party with an anti-Catholic nativist posture, the Democratic party and the Democratic political machine were the most obvious sources of ethnic power. For "bosses" who normally were of working-class origin and who could not retreat to the management of a family bank or business when out of office, the winning, keeping, and using of political power became virtually an end in itself. Survival by staying in power was the name of the game, not any abstract commitment to providing "the best government for the least money" or to achieving civic reform "with benefits for all on an equalitarian basis." But if the machine organization provided stability in an urban society in a state of flux, where even native Americans were bewildered by social situations they did not fully understand and immigrants were in even greater confusion, it also exacted a price for its favors, its jobs, its charities, and its spectacles. "What it did for the poor," D. W. Brogan remarks, "may have been far less than what it did against them, but what it did was very visible; what it did against them was usually, though not always, invisible. . . ."[4]

As time went by, the favors the machine could offer were rivaled by those given by other political organizations—notably the federal government. With the Depression, machine charity collapsed like most other forms of organized charity, and with the New Deal and subsequent social legislation, voters began to receive as a right more than they had ever received as a favor from the "bosses." Machine politics—which had long viewed "honest graft" as simply a political version of what businessmen

[4] D. W. Brogan, *Politics in America* (New York: Harper Brothers, 1954), p. 129.

routinely engaged in when they used inside information to make speculative gains—was increasingly driven over the border into "plain" or "dirty graft," whose profits came from the toleration of crime and vice. Because the business of the machines had been the pragmatic manipulation of power, they had been more occupied with winning and holding that power than with the creation of broadly based social programs. "Only gradually," William Shannon points out, "did the social discipline grow to meet the power and only when that happened did the majority detach themselves from the values of the political machine."[5]

Mayor Richard J. Daley of Chicago was, until his death in 1976, the last fully realized example of the big-city Irish "boss." His political style and the political machine he dominated were the end products of a century of Irish urban political life and a prime example of what that unique Irish political style had involved. Daley spent his whole life climbing the rungs of the political ladder. In the Democratic party hierarchy he had begun as a precinct worker in his own 11th Ward, advanced to ward secretary, ward committeeman, and finally to county chairman. In government positions he had progressed from the state house of representatives, to state senate, to director of revenue for Illinois, to county clerk of Cook County and finally to the mayoralty in 1955. Throughout his long climb he was guided by a set of values that were consistent with his view of Chicago as a city of neighborhood communities where God-fearing and hard working people should take care of their own problems and help each other, and where the acceptance of responsibility and uncompromising morality (as he defined it) should be guidelines for conducting personal as well as public affairs. Daley was the epitome of the Irish political style that had dominated American urban life for over a century.

Milton N. Rakove, whose research on Daley's Chicago machine included a stint as participant-observer working in the machine, has provided a perceptive analysis of these values that guided Daley and motivated his passion for, and success in, politics.[6] Deeply conservative, Rakove says, Daley exemplified "the old-line Irish Catholic acceptance of a world in which life is harsh, problems are normal, man is sinful, and struggle and hard work are necessary to obtain a foothold in this world and to improve one's status in society."[7] To survive, men must combine a strenuous effort to raise themselves by their own bootstraps with a responsibility to help their fellowmen if they have also tried hard but have been less successful. Daley's world view was a parochial one, for he never moved from his Irish Catholic neighborhood of Bridgeport where he had been raised, married, raised his children, and where he was finally buried. When Daley insisted in the 1960s that there were no ghettos in Chicago—only neigh-

[5] Shannon, *The American Irish,* p. 64.

[6] Milton L. Rakove, *Don't Make No Waves, Don't Back No Losers: An Insider's Analysis of the Daley Machine* (Bloomington: Indiana University Press, 1975), pp. 60–75.

[7] *Ibid.,* p. 62.

borhoods—he spoke with the insider's perception that home is not a ghetto to the person who lives there, whatever liberal reformers may call it. Daley's moral view included the belief that the purpose of politics was to try to make men behave as morally as possible while still accepting the fact that they probably could not and would not be particularly moral. He saw a certain amount of corruption in government as inevitable and to be lamented, but as long as people were not apostates, heretics, or adulterers he accepted the fact that sinful behavior was part of the human condition.

In his political actions, Daley is described by Rakove as a master both of political technique and of administrative skills, whose goal was not social reform so much as ministering to people's wants and needs on an individual basis and getting out the votes to ensure that he would be in a position to continue doing so. Unable to understand the point of view of the latest immigrants to Chicago—the black and Spanish-speaking minorities—except through his own familiar perception that welfare had always in the past been a gift, not a right, and that if things went badly for a group it was more that society and government were inefficient than that they were unjust, he still did not consider himself an "old style " politician but simply a professional who played the game of politics as it had always been played and would always be played. For politicians such as Daley, Rakove concluded, "problems are hardly ever solved and great social movements always fall short of achieving their objectives. In their world, pragmatism, tolerance, and humility are the marks of the successful practitioners of the craft."[8]

Daley was a successful, and thoroughly Irish, practitioner of the craft of politics. In the last years of his reign over Chicago politics, the Democratic Central Committee headed by Daley and composed of fifty ward committeemen along with thirty suburban township committeemen, each responsible for precinct captains and their assistants, controlled over 25,000 government patronage jobs—fewer than during the 1930s and 1940s because of civil service jobs that had been removed from the patronage list, but still an impressive figure.[9] The machine could count on political and economic support from organized labor and from the steady flow of contributions from the lowest to the highest levels of voters whose lives were influenced by the bounty or by the threat of the machine. "Out of this vast amalgam of patronage, money, special interests, restrictive election laws, and organizational discipline," says Mike Royko in his portrait of Daley's Chicago machine, "emerge a handful of candidates, and they are supposed to be what it is all about."[10] Whether in Chicago, or in other cities where machines had developed to meet the singular needs of the individually

[8] *Ibid.*, p. 74.

[9] *Ibid.*, p. 113.

[10] Mike Royko, *Boss: Richard J. Daley of Chicago* (New York: New American Library, 1971), p. 77.

powerless to assert group strength, and where people had felt that a vote was a "simple favor" to give in exchange for security, the election of machine candidates had indeed been what it was all about. Daley's death in 1976 marked the belated end of an era which had been uniquely American and uniquely Irish.

With all its failings, machine politics had channeled the Irish drive for power into legitimate political avenues and had provided upward mobility in a profession that was highly honored among those Irish who had been denied political power in their homeland. Corrupt as the machines may have been from the standpoint of Anglo-Americans, the Irish saw them as functioning systems of power and necessary channels for the redistribution of wealth under conditions where it was clear that power would be wielded by someone. The shift away from local ethnic power coalitions to national power, with its emphasis on rationality and broadly conceived laws, led to a gradual decline of the urban party machine. The dominance of the Irish in machine politics actually outlived their numerical and electoral strength in the cities, as increasing numbers moved to suburban areas, and now as the last of the Irish machine politicians work their way through the hierarchy of power, it is members of other ethnic groups who assume leadership under changed conditions. Meanwhile, where party patronage jobs have dwindled, those fortunate enough to come by such positions cling to them in such cities as Chicago and Boston, providing what Brogan describes as "the last vestiges of the old party system as a reminder of the role once performed by urban immigrant groups and the leaders who directed them."[11]

Whether, on balance, the era of the Irish big-city "bosses" will be viewed as a creative, if somewhat limited, adaptation of ethnic needs to American political processes, or whether machine politics will be viewed as a political perversion which induced the Irish to trade petty favors for votes that could have been more wisely cast, remains to be seen. The power of the machines had been used to eliminate discriminatory anti-Catholic patterns in schools, jails, and hospitals, to appoint the Irish to public jobs in education and in the police and fire departments, and to provide security for large numbers of fellow Irish as well as for loyal machine supporters from other ethnic groups.

Not until the twentieth century were the Irish seriously challenged in their urban political power, but the residue of earlier work kept them in command in countless cities for another half century at least. Looking back on the era of Irish dominance over urban politics, Lawrence McCaffrey observes that paradoxically it has been their "conservative, skeptical, often cynical attitude toward man and his environment [that] has made the Irish more successful as practical reformers than ideological liberals have been," for when it finally became apparent that government had an obligation to

[11] Brogan, *Politics in America,* p. 45.

provide for the social security of its citizens "it was the Irish politicians in cities, not Anglo-American Protestant leaders in suburban or rural America, who served as the core of minority group coalitions that made possible the New Deal, Fair Deal, New Frontier, and the Great Society."[12] Thus McCaffrey sees the Irish as bridging the gap between Roman Catholic and Anglo-Saxon Protestant cultures, leading other Catholic ethnics into accommodation with American political styles, and in the process "pushing a reluctant United States along the road to the welfare state."[13] The transition from a bucket of coal or a job provided by the bounty of the machine to a social security check or a retraining program provided by the government may seem great, but the perception that the role of government is to help out in an imperfect world is much the same.

Before we toll the death knell of the big-city political machines, however, it is worth noting that other ethnic minorities may use essentially the same techniques the Irish used to rise to power in community politics. Rakove's analysis of Daley's Chicago machine in 1975 suggests that the machine provides:

> a classic laboratory and a political system which could serve as a pragmatic model of successful politics in an American city. For whatever criticisms have been leveled at the Chicago machine, even by its most severe critics, the durability of the machine, its efficiency, and its ability to survive and prosper, despite the urban crisis, cannot be challenged.[14]

He goes on to predict that the era of machine politics may not yet have run its course, and is not likely soon to be replaced by "nonpartisan, reform, public-regarding, problem-oriented urban political systems," but that instead the inheritors of urban political power may be the pragmatic, power-seeking politicians of the emerging black and Spanish-speaking communities who will have the same goals and use the same techniques as did the ethnic bosses of an earlier day. If that happens, he concludes, the machine will survive as "a model of things to come in America, rather than a vestigial curiosity of things past."[15]

## POLITICAL PRESSURE FOR A FREE IRELAND

During the years of growing Irish political influence in America, the "Irish question" remained an unresolved problem. By the 1880s, Britain recognized that the Irish drive for freedom was no longer a national move-

[12] Lawrence J. McCaffrey, *The Irish Diaspora in America* (Bloomington: Indiana University Press, 1976), p. 150.

[13] *Ibid.,* p. 151.

[14] Rakove, *Don't Make No Waves,* p. 3.

[15] *Ibid.,* p. 18.

ment but had become an international issue, as American Irish provided a haven for exiled nationalist leaders as well as money and political pressure. The Irish American press served as the chief instrument for keeping nationalist issues before the immigrants, but family legends perpetuated both fervent affection for a country reluctantly left behind and intense hatred for the despised British who were held responsible for the forced emigration. Thus, the sentiment, the leadership, and the information were available to those American Irish who wished to exert pressure for a free Ireland, but a lack of consensus about the best means to achieve their goal limited the potential effectiveness of Irish American pressure to certain critical periods in American political life.

The period of the Civil War provided the first occasion for recognizing the potential impact of Irish voting power on American foreign policy. British-American relations were already strained by Confederate use of Canada as a sanctuary from which to attack Union forces during the War. At the end of hostilities, American anti-British sentiment was such that the militant Fenians felt encouraged to launch an invasion of Canada with the object of forcing England to abandon her age-old domination of Ireland. Thomas Brown describes the three-way political struggle represented by the Fenian assault on Canada:

> The nationalist leaders in Ireland thought all this an American madness, but it suited the needs of American politics. The administrations of both Johnson and Grant tolerated the Fenians because their vote was feared, and the Secretary of State, Seward, thought their pugnacity provided him with a useful weapon in bargaining with the British Foreign Office. In the scramble for power that developed during Reconstruction years the politicians exploited the Fenians, and the Fenians, in turn, did their best to exploit the politicians.[16]

Although the Fenian assaults—on Canada, and later on Ireland—failed, their new-found awareness of Irish voting strength was a heady experience for immigrants so recently arrived in America. Meanwhile, during the 1860s, the British Parliament had removed two of the more serious Irish grievances by passing the Irish Land Act and disestablishing the Church of Ireland, and had encouraged the less militant Irish both at home and in America to believe that parliamentary methods could be effective, given the existence of political pressure on England to make concessions. From that point on, the Irish became aware of the benefits of cohesiveness and the power of their vote in influencing Congress, the White House, and the State Department during periods when they could determine the balance of power in American politics.

Such a period emerged again in the 1880s, when Charles Stewart Parnell led the Irish Catholics during their struggles for Home Rule and

[16] Brown, *Irish-American Nationalism,* p. 40.

against the Irish land system. The Irish land war of 1880–81 captured the imagination of American Irish and, through over 1200 local chapters of the Land League in America, over $100,000 had been sent to Ireland by 1881. Not only did general sympathy for Ireland lead state legislatures to pass resolutions condemning British actions in Ireland, but many Irish supporters returned to Ireland to take part in what they hoped would be the last battle against Britain. When the Americans were jailed along with Irish revolutionaries without right of trial by jury, prominent members of Congress interceded to bring pressure through the White House and State Department to have the Americans of Irish descent freed. Under pressure, the British capitulated to American demands and agreed to free all Irish American prisoners, provided they would leave Ireland. Irish influence had operated on two levels: Radical agitation had enlisted money and the direct support of small numbers of American Irish who returned to Ireland to aid in the Irish struggles but, more importantly, Irish political pressure at the American national level had forced the British to free American nationals.

The years between 1910 and 1923 saw a third period during which Irish Americans exerted pressure on the national government to help resolve the Irish question. At the outbreak of World War I, there was strong anti-British sentiment among Irish Americans, further churned up by German propagandists, while in Ireland leaders of the abortive Easter Rebellion attempted to take advantage of England's preoccupation with the war in Europe. After quickly crushing the rebellion, the British outraged Irish and Anglo-Americans alike by executing the nationalist leaders. In spite of anti-British feeling, the majority of Irish Americans gave wholehearted support to the war effort after the United States entry in 1917; yet in the same year 134 members of the House of Representatives cabled the British Prime Minister urging settlement of the Irish question. Versailles saw no mention of Irish independence, an omission for which Irish Americans held Woodrow Wilson largely responsible, and both Irish and Irish Americans were torn between those insisting on freedom for all of Ireland and the British offer of dominion status for all but the six most heavily Protestant counties of Ulster in Northern Ireland. At length, the competing factions agreed to work within a system that would provide for an Irish Free State to include all but the six northern counties. The vast majority of American Irish were satisfied that they had made a significant contribution to resolving the ancient Irish problem.

In the years after the creation of the Irish Free State, Irish American involvement in Irish affairs has largely evaporated as the American Irish have turned their attention to full involvement in American life. In retrospect, Irish American nationalist activity, which takes on the appearance of a recurrent motif in the American political mosaic, may be best characterized as a movement that served to consolidate voting strength within the

Irish community. The sense of common cause in defense of Irish freedom was a vehicle that permitted experimentation in politics and that remained an important corollary of political power in the first two decades of this century.

Half a century later, when Northern Ireland became convulsed with civil strife in the 1970s, the American Irish were too far removed from the need that existed earlier to become deeply involved in Irish affairs. Although the British Government estimates that as much as 85 percent of the arms flowing to the Irish Republican Army in Northern Ireland are bought in America with American-donated money, and that $2,000,000 to $3,000,000 in aid for dependents of I.R.A. men is provided by Americans, except for those Irish who immigrated in the two decades after World War II, there seems little evidence that the majority of American Irish are willing to commit themselves to the struggle in Northern Ireland beyond the gesture of contributing to the "cause" when the hat is passed after the singing of Irish songs in an Irish American bar. "As Americans," William Shannon points out, "they have the security to perceive the complexity of the Ulster problem and to view it from an emotional distance." He concludes that entering fully into the passions that convulse Northern Ireland "would require a journey into the past they are reluctant to make. They are too involved with the American present and future."[17]

## THE NEW STYLE IN IRISH CATHOLIC POLITICS

The transition from the old to the new style in Irish political behavior and goals after the 1930s was a product of changes in the cities, changes in the Irish, and changes in the political benefits that could be offered. The Irish began to move physically and emotionally—hence politically as well—beyond the ethnically enclosed neighborhood. Alfred Smith, the Democratic nominee for President in 1928, had come up from Lower Manhattan through Tammany Hall to become a distinguished and long-term Governor of New York State, and his overwhelming defeat by Hoover represented a bitter defeat for the Irish. Religion was probably a factor in that defeat, but his stand against prohibition and his progressive record in Albany also contributed to his rejection by American voters. He was a man emerging directly from the big-city machine, and suspect partly for that reason. But in the subsequent decade, Franklin Roosevelt and the New Deal provided opportunities for Irish Americans at the national level, where Thomas Walsh and later Frank Murphy served as Attorney General, James Farley as Postmaster General and party manager, Thomas Corcoran

[17] William Shannon, "The Lasting Hurrah," *The New York Times Magazine,* March 14, 1976, p. 78.

as presidential advisor, John McCormack as strategist in the House of Representatives, and Joseph Kennedy as Ambassador to Britain. World War II brought full Irish support for the war effort, although the Irish Free State itself remained neutral.

By the 1950s, Senator Joseph McCarthy was sowing dissension in the Irish community and fear among Americans generally with his flamboyant accusations of Communist activities at high levels of government. A Republican from Wisconsin, McCarthy was outside the discipline of machine politics which, for all its other weaknesses, still would not have tolerated the individual grandstanding that was McCarthy's characteristic style. By the very nature of his attacks, he seemed to imply two things that struck sympathetic chords in the minds of many Irish Catholics: that only devout Catholics could fully appreciate the threat to religion that communism represented, and that the wellborn and well educated Anglo-Americans who had been posing as models of propriety all these years were among the least loyal of all Americans. In Shannon's view,

> McCarthyism was a major crisis in the coming of age of the Irish Catholic community in the United States. It derived strength from the worst, the weakest, and the most outdated parts of the Irish experience in this country. But it also evoked and tested the best in that experience. It was fed by old parochialisms, old prejudices, old misunderstandings. But it was also combated by growing sophistication and deepening moral and political maturity.[18]

The image of the Irish as anti-civil-libertarians in the McCarthy mold received little support from studies made in the 1950s, and still less support from NORC studies in the 1970s.[19] If McCarthy derived his strength from the worst, the weakest, and the most outdated parts of the Irish experience in this country, his opponents—Eugene McCarthy and Bishop Sheil, for example—drew strength from another part of that experience. It was that more positive side which coalesced in the person of the Irish American candidate for the presidency in the election of 1960.

While he undoubtedly benefited from the organizational strength of the Democratic political machines in which the Irish had invested so much, John F. Kennedy was above all a man whom Americans could accept as a performer who could operate in terms of a generally accepted code of democratic political principles. The voters believed him when he assured them he would take a neutral stance both with regard to his Catholicism and his ethnic group, and that he would be his own man in the highly specialized job of the presidency. As he well knew, an Irish Catholic candidate would have to overcome enormous difficulties, first to win the nomination, then the election, and success would demand a concentrated effort by the entire

[18] Shannon, *The American Irish,* p. 381.

[19] Andrew M. Greeley, *The American Catholic: A Social Portrait* (New York: Basic Books, Inc.,1977), pp. 104–5.

Irish political community. To do this would require acceptance by the big-city Irish political figures and confidence on their part that entrenched power would be undisturbed.

Kennedy had the polish born of wealth and superior education, and was little damaged by the stereotypes of Irish political style that had attached to Alfred Smith, yet he was close enough to the political experience of the Irish in America to make use of the powerful Irish base of political power that had been developing over the years. Insisting that he was not the "Catholic candidate," he explicitly faced the issue of separation of church and state in his speech before the American Protestant ministers in Houston, Texas, in 1960 when he said: "I do not speak for my church on public matters—and the church does not speak for me."[20] Whether Kennedy proved to be a less committed Catholic than Protestants had feared he would be, or whether Protestants had, by and large, become aware of the fallacies in their own ethnocentric religious thinking, there was nothing in the Kennedy presidency to evoke religious alarm. Catholicism, as practiced by this intellectually confident Irish Catholic President, was no longer the threat it had once been.

Kennedy did not receive all of the Irish Catholic vote. By some of the American Irish he was even perceived as being more WASP than Irish. But there was no question that his success was of monumental satisfaction for Irish Americans as for other Catholic ethnics, who had agreed with him when warned that if the election was to be decided on the basis that 40 million Americans lost their chance of being President on the day they were baptized, then it would be the whole nation that would be the loser. The salience of ethnicity was probably at a temporarily high level in those months just before Kennedy's election. Since his presidency, however, the issue of Catholicism has scarcely emerged as a question worth raising in national presidential politics.

If Kennedy made visible a new liberal Irish Catholic style in politics, the decade of the 1960s further accentuated the end of a political era in which the Irish had played so important a part. Cities were inundated with complex problems involving other ethnic minorities; the orderly world represented by machine politics seemed to crumble; religious bonds were dramatically affected by the less separatist and more ecumenical spirit emerging from Vatican II. In the aftermath of the 1960s, the Irish Catholic political style is clearly no longer that of the old-style "boss." Indeed, if there is *a* style, it is as varied as the range of social and intellectual positions the Irish have come to occupy in America today.

But as both politicians and voters move into a new period in American politics, there is continuing evidence of a characteristic Irish approach, if no longer a specific style. National Opinion Research Center studies show that the Irish still have the highest overall political participation of any ethnic group in the country, and that they are characteristically politi-

[20] *New York Times,* September 13, 1960, p. 22.

cal activists as measured by campaigning and political contributions.[21] They are more likely than either Jews or Anglo-Americans to be involved in community political organizations, to vote, and to keep in personal contact with their political leaders, but their approach to political affairs in all these respects comes closer to that of both Jews and Anglo-Americans than it does to that of other Catholic ethnic groups.

This modified style, combined with the highest level of overall political participation of any ethnic group in the country, appears a natural outcome of the movement away from ethnic neighborhoods, the increase in higher education, and the broader view of political responsibility. What is not so self-evident is the continuing enthusiasm of the Irish for political involvement, a concern that has outlived the solution of those early problems that political activism was intended to relieve.

Clearly, the Irish, more than any other American immigrant group, have always perceived politics as the most accessible avenue to social mobility and the most direct route to power. "They really leaped into the power thing," an Irish American educator commented recently, and continued:

> I wonder whether that is because power, in a political sense, is a word business—an oral tradition. Words are what the Irish are best at. Skilled oral dueling. It's a much admired affair still in Ireland, where one finds people of very limited education, doing what we would consider very nonverbal jobs, who are extremely verbal people—speaking and using just the correct word, and holding the floor and debating, whether in a pub or wherever.[22]

Centuries of practice in developing an oral tradition, under an English rule that denied access both to the written tradition and to full political participation in their own affairs, certainly had not been wasted on the Catholic Irish. When the opportunity arose in America, they were already overqualified and anxious to "leap into the power thing."

Perhaps because of experience with what they had considered an illegitimate British government in Ireland, the Irish adopted the legitimate American political structure with a special enthusiasm, and learned early how to influence political decisions at the local level where their effects would be most immediately felt. Surely the need for political contributions and for campaign workers has never been doubted by the American Irish, who support candidates with time and money unmatched by any other ethnic group. Historically, the costs of political participation in Ireland were always high, and the risks great. Whatever the price in America, it has been lower and the rewards greater than they had come to expect in Ireland.

[21] Greeley, *The American Catholic,* pp. 104–5.

[22] Private conversation with Thomas E. O'Connell, President of Berkshire Community College, August 1976.

# CHAPTER NINE

# Irish Americans and the Catholic Church

The relationship between the Irish and the Catholic Church is a recurring theme in any discussion of the Irish experience. Both in the support that the faith gave to a disheartened and downtrodden people during years of subjugation in their homeland and in the continuity of tradition that the parishes and their priests provided in those difficult early years in America, Catholicism was a basic part of Irish identity. As the first of the large waves of Catholic immigrants to arrive in America after the mid-1880s, the Irish, along with lesser numbers of German Catholics, successfully established Catholicism as a minority religion that could stand its ground in a predominantly Protestant country. Daniel Moynihan, writing in 1963, referred to the role of the Irish in transforming their Church from a despised and proscripted sect of the eighteenth century to the largest religious organization in the nation as "incomparably the most important thing they have done in America" although he went on to add that "they have done it at a price."[1]

To set the stage for discussion of the current relationship between today's Irish Americans and the Catholic Church their forefathers helped to establish, several points should be recalled from previous chapters. First, although political and economic factors had been at the root of England's desire to subdue the Irish and keep Ireland in a dependent colonial position, it was their Catholicism to which the Irish could attribute their "separateness" from the dominating British. The clergy, in this embattled situation, had been able to develop close and personal ties with the peasantry at the parish level but had maintained only relatively weak ties with Roman Catholicism. Because the Irish upper classes had fled to other countries, the sophistication and aristocratic temper that characterized Roman Catholicism elsewhere in Europe had been largely lost in Ireland. It had become a defensive peasant religion.

Second, recall that the largely Protestant Irish who had emigrated to America before 1830 had already established themselves at various social

[1] Nathan Glazer and Daniel P. Moynihan, *Beyond the Melting Pot* (Cambridge: MIT Press, 1970), p. 230.

class levels before the arrival of the famine immigrants at mid-century. It was this later famine migration that provided the negative stereotypes of the Irish as both culturally and religiously offensive to Protestant Americans. The subsequent decision to establish a separate Catholic school system, parallel to the emerging public schools, implied that Catholics not only intended to remain different by choice and commitment but that they wished to socialize their children differently from those of the Protestant majority.

Third, in communities where there were sufficiently large numbers of Irish Catholics, the formation of ethnic neighborhoods with parallel Irish social organizations indicated that cultural assimilation during the first generation or two had not automatically ensured movement into Anglo Protestant society on a primary group level, even for those upwardly mobile Irish who might have wished it. For Protestants and Catholics alike, it was not so much the specifically Irish component of ethnicity as it was the specifically Catholic component that served to maintain the barriers and foster structural pluralism.

Finally, recall from our discussion of SuperNORC and other research in Chapter 5 that Irish Catholics have now caught up with, and in many areas surpassed, the average accomplishments of Protestant Americans with whom they compared so unfavorably during those early years. Significant also is the fact that they have maintained a strong commitment to Catholicism as well as some characteristic attitudes and values that differ in important ways from those of Protestant Americans. While the Irish Catholic subsociety with its parallel institutions and ethnic communality still exists at some class levels and in some places, there is growing evidence that the boundaries are permeable and that Irish Catholics are increasingly merging at their own class levels with Catholics of other ethnic minorities and with members of the Protestant majority.

In *Irish American-Nationalism*, Thomas N. Brown observed that "perhaps the greatest difficulty which confronts the historians of the Irish is that of differentiating between the specifically Irish and specifically Catholic aspects of their lives. They had emerged into the modern world from a past in which Catholicism had played perhaps a stronger role than for any other people of Western Europe."[2] The sociologist faces the same dilemma as the historian. It is perhaps impossible to separate the part played by Catholicism in creating a social context for belief and action in a largely Protestant country from the part played by the Irish cultural heritage in which that Catholicism has been embedded; but in an attempt to make the separation this chapter will consider the Irish role in the development of the Catholic Church in America, the impact of Catholic education on Irish American

[2] Thomas N. Brown, *Irish-American Nationalism* (New York: J. B. Lippincott Co., 1966), p. 34.

social mobility and intellectual life, and the effects of liberalizing changes in the Catholic Church in the wake of the Second Vatican Council.

## THE ROLE OF THE IRISH IN ESTABLISHING THE AMERICAN CATHOLIC CHURCH

Before the Irish arrived in large numbers in the mid-nineteenth century, American Catholics were too few in number to raise alarm among the Protestant majority.[3] In the late 1700s, the total Catholic population was little more than 30,000, under the authority of a single bishop and served by only 30 priests. By 1820, the number had risen to roughly a quarter of a million Catholics, and by 1830 to three-quarters of a million. Before the impact of the famine Irish, Lawrence McCaffrey notes, "American Catholics were culturally Anglo-Saxon, and like their English counterparts they were humble and quiet in their religious observances, tiptoeing about so as not to disturb or antagonize the Protestant majority."[4] Small in number, inconspicuous, and respected, the early Catholic leaders (many of whom, like John Carroll, the first American Catholic bishop, were of Irish origin themselves) cultivated a style of Catholicism that would merge into the mainstream of Anglo-American culture. But the famine years changed all that.

Within the short span of three decades, a massive religious explosion had occurred in America. From a membership of under 1,000,000 in 1830, Catholics numbered over 3,000,000 by 1860. The vast majority of these were Irish whose religious and social characteristics were in striking contrast to those of the existing Catholic population. Fearing that the aggressive and culturally unsophisticated Irish would incur the wrath of native-born Catholics, Ambrose Marechal, the Frenchman who had succeeded Carroll as head of the American Catholic Church, and who sympathized with Carroll's vision of a distinctly American Catholicism, complained of the unreliability of the Irish priests. Those missionary priests who had accompanied the immigrants to America had been, in fact, among the least disciplined and most unruly of the Irish ecclesiastics and were frequently almost as culturally and intellectually unpolished as their parishioners.

Yet the sheer numbers of the Irish, their concentration in urban areas, and their demand for Irish clergy inevitably led to the transformation of

[3] For further information on the role of the Irish in the development of the American Catholic Church, see the following works, on which this chapter draws heavily: John Cogley, *Catholic America,* (New York: The Dial Press, 1973), Ch. 2–3; and Lawrence J. McCaffrey, *The Irish Diaspora in America* (Bloomington: Indiana University Press, 1976), Ch. 6.

[4] McCaffrey, *The Irish Diaspora in America*, p. 89.

the Catholic Church in America from an institution under native-born and French leadership to one primarily Irish and urban-based. Subsequent Irish bishops took steps to ensure that the quality of the priests sent from Ireland was improved, and hastened to build seminaries for the education of priests in America. But despite these concessions, American Catholicism had been imprinted with a different stamp from the one chosen by the Church's earlier leaders. From this point on, McCaffrey observes, "American Catholicism became and for a long time remained part of an Irish-Catholic religious empire that dominated the English-speaking world."[5]

In religion, as in so much else, the famine period provided the catalyst for change both in Ireland and in America. Not only lives, but institutions as well, were structured differently in the aftermath of the famine. Prior to the 1850s, Irish Catholicism had been loosely structured, closely identified with the daily life of the Irish peasants, and more sensitive to Irish needs than to Vatican policy. It was a rural, richly communal, traditional, peasant religion, stripped of the cultural richness normally associated with Catholicism. If it contrasted sharply with the emerging form of American Catholicism, it was equally anathema to the reforms that were to be introduced to Ireland in the 1870s by Paul Cardinal Cullen in a successful effort to instill authority and discipline in the Catholic Church in Ireland.Thus 1870 marks the point at which Irishmen both at home and in their new environment were exposed to rigid religious controls over morals and conduct that came to typify a new puritanism within Roman Catholicism. This new morally austere and puritanical approach accommodated itself much more easily to the Victorian Protestantism which surrounded the Irish in their populous settlements in the urban Northeast.

A somewhat different pattern was developing in the Midwest, where German Catholics put more emphasis on intellectualism and Irish bishops urged greater accommodation to American life and culture. However, it was the powerful urban concentration of Irish in the East that had, by the late 1800s, established dominance over the American Catholic Church, and over the spreading institutional network of hospitals, orphanages, schools, and colleges that it supported. This fact had enormous consequences for the assimilation of later Catholic ethnic groups into Anglo-American society. The dominance of the Irish in the development of American Catholicism meant that Protestant Americans would have their first real encounter with Catholics under rather atypical circumstances and that they would inevitably associate the cultural attributes of the Irish peasant with those of Catholicism. In 1853, when Archbishop Cajetan Bedini was sent on an official visit to survey the state of Catholicism in America, he understood the sociological implications of this situation well enough to report back to the Vatican that Americans had contact only with poor, igno-

[5] Ibid., p. 91.

rant, lower-class Irishmen, which, he concluded, went far in explaining why there was such widespread antipathy to Catholicism.[6] By the time the Irish and their later, more disciplined form of Catholicism had taken root in America, however, the first indelible impressions had been made. Noteworthy, too, is the fact that even today, although Irish Americans represent less than 20 percent of all American Catholics, 30 percent of the clergy and over half the hierarchy remain Irish.[7]

In purely secular terms, the awesome investment in their religious life has meant that for a century the Irish have contributed time, money, and talent which a less religiously committed group might have invested in other pursuits. Viewed another way, the investment has meant that the Irish Catholic subsociety has nurtured the talents of its members from within its own institutions. Only since World War II have sustantial numbers of the urban Irish chosen to abandon the city parishes they once occupied, and to make the move to suburban areas where the institutions are less readily available. In the process, more of the young have chosen careers in business and the professions rather than in the religious life—a situation which has prompted some Irish Catholics to observe that you could always count on the Irish, more than the Italians or any other group, to become priests or nuns, but today one cannot count on the Irish anymore. The consequences of this change are nowhere to be felt more than in the staffing of the Catholic elementary and secondary schools, which were developed and maintained through the years largely by Irish Catholics and which were so basic to their urban communities.

## CATHOLIC EDUCATION AND SOCIAL MOBILITY

When, in 1884, the Third Plenary Council of the American Hierarchy of the Catholic Church directed each parish to set up a parish school and admonished Catholic parents to send their children to such schools, the Council was reacting defensively to changing patterns in American education that were perceived as threatening the faith of the predominantly Irish Catholic children of school age.[8] The "common schools" of the 1700s had been locally supported and controlled, and reflected the religious doctrines of the communities they served. As religious homogeneity began to break down in the early 1800s, with Irish immigration and Protestant

[6] Cogley, *Catholic America,* p. 48.

[7] Andrew M. Greeley, *The American Catholic: A Social Portrait* (New York: Basic Books, Inc., 1977), p. 26.

[8] For further discussion of the early development of American public education and of parochial schools see Andrew Greeley and Peter Rossi, *The Education of Catholic Americans* (Chicago: Aldine, 1966), Ch. 1; and Michael B. Katz, *Class, Bureaucracy, and Schools: The Illusion of Educational Change in America* rev. ed. (New York: Praeger, 1975), Ch. 1.

schisms, state and local governments began to adopt the principle of universal, publicly supported, compulsory education. Although these schools subscribed to no particular religious doctrine they had a strong Protestant bias, and in many Irish parishes the pressure to send children to such schools was interpreted as both patronizing and proselytizing.

As American public education, itself a relatively new phenomenon in the mid-1800s, attempted to deal with the problem of ever increasing numbers of immigrant children and the questions of religious orientation and of centralized versus local control, at least two theoretical models emerged as possibilities. The pluralist model, proposed in 1840 by New York Governor William Seward to the state legislature,[9] would have permitted immigrant children to be taught in schools by teachers who spoke the same languages and professed the same faith. Although, at most, probably no more than one-third of Irish children spoke Irish (Gaelic) rather than English, even at that early date, such a model would have opened the way for schools in which the native cultures and religions of other groups would be retained. At the other extreme, the assimilationist model, in line with the schools as they were then developing, would have enforced cultural and religious assimilation through funding only those schools which reflected the Anglo-American culture and taught the Protestant faith. The pluralist model was acceptable to Catholics. The assimilationist model was acceptable to Protestants.

Neither Catholics nor Protestants were pleased by the compromise model that eventually was adopted. According to this solution, cultural assimilation would proceed within a presumably classless and religiously neutral school system. Since both Catholics and Protestants felt that religious education had a place in the school, it was a compromise by which both sides lost. Catholics, however, lost most, for at that time instructional materials were heavily biased toward a Protestant outlook. Given the teachers and the texts at hand, there was simply no way to make the schools religiously neutral. With Irish immigration rapidly increasing, the fear grew among Catholics that American Catholicism could survive only by preserving the faith in the security of a separate school system, even if this must be maintained at great sacrifice by the Catholic community. While the goal of a parish school for each American parish was never met, the Catholic Church did develop and maintain the most extensive, non-governmentally funded denominational school system to be found in any modern country. About 50 percent of American Catholic children have been able to receive at least some part of their education in church-supported schools.[10]

Through the 1950s, the vast network of parochial schools in urban areas was maintained, staffed, and attended largely by Irish Catholics.

[9] Glazer and Moynihan, *Beyond the Melting Pot,* p. 235.
[10] Greeley and Rossi, *The Education of Catholic Americans,* p. 24.

Here second-, third-, and later generation Irish Americans were being assimilated into the American culture, taught marketable skills, and purged of their peasant heritage, in addition to being taught to obey the strictures of the church. Inevitably, questions arose in Protestant minds about the quality of education in Catholic schools, and in time Catholics themselves wondered whether the additional financial burden of maintaining a separate school system could be justified by evidence that would show that this was indeed the only, or best, way to protect the faith of Catholic children.

Because parochial schools operated outside the public realm, they had been largely beyond the reach and concern of those academic measuring instruments so widely used to gauge progress in public school systems, but in Protestant eyes it was widely assumed that Catholic education was almost willfully inferior. Of all America's gifts, public education—along with the presumed opportunities it would make available—has long been considered the greatest. Not only was it the surest path to social mobility but it was the great homogenizer which would bring together people of different ethnic and social class backgrounds. It was, therefore, viewed as suspect when a minority group voluntarily rejected access to that same school system and established its own separate and parallel schools in the belief that they were somehow preferable.

The social and religious questions raised in Protestant and Catholic minds about the effectiveness and the consequences of Catholic education were investigated in two studies whose results were published in 1966. The Carnegie-sponsored Notre Dame survey, *Catholic Schools in Action,* used standard tests which showed that 84 percent of elementary students in Catholic Schools achieved scores at or above national norms, and 17 percent of high school students exceeded the national norms in academic areas (with more than 80 percent classified as reaching their full potential in language, math, science, and social science.)[11] In the National Opinion Research Center (NORC) study, *The Education of American Catholics,* Andrew Greeley and Peter Rossi focused on the impact of Catholic education on religious behavior and social attitudes. For the 44 percent of Catholic children attending parochial schools in the mid-1960s (of whom about 18 percent were Irish), the religious impact of parochial education was found to be greatest among those who attended these schools from first grade through college, and who came from devout Catholic homes. Greeley and Rossi concluded, however, that "there is no evidence that Catholic schools have been necessary for the survival of American Catholicism."[12] Thus, academically, parochial schools were found to be roughly comparable to public schools, and, in terms of religion, to have the greatest impact upon those who already came from devout homes and who attended the

[11] Reginald H. Neuwein (Ed.), *Catholic Schools in Action* (Notre Dame: University of Notre Dame Press, 1966).

[12] Greeley and Rossi, *The Education of Catholic Americans,* p. 221.

longest. In terms of social attitudes, the NORC survey provided evidence that Catholic children who had attended parochial schools were no more clannish and were generally more liberal in their social and political attitudes than those who had attended public schools. In addition, alumni of Catholic colleges were more likely to have excelled in the professions than those from non-Catholic colleges.

In a separate analysis of the Irish Catholics in the 1963–64 NORC Parochial School Study, Harold Abramson found that the 18 percent of Irish in the sample were more likely to have attended Catholic high schools than the sample's Catholic population as a whole, and were almost twice as likely to have gone on to some kind of college.[13] The reasons were largely socioeconomic, for in the years immediately preceding the NORC study the Irish had reached that point in the assimilation process where they were fully aware of the importance of education for social mobility, anxious still to preserve both their Catholic and their Irish identities in a Catholic environment, and able to afford the high tuitions demanded by Catholic secondary schools that were clearly superior to urban public schools as college preparatory institutions. Indeed, by the end of World War II, returning Irish Catholic veterans could take extraordinarily effective advantage of the opportunities provided in the G.I. Bill. It was precisely at this time that Irish Catholics for the first time were sending a higher percentage of students on to colleges than any ethnic group except the Jews. Among British Protestants 42 percent attended college in the post-World War II group; the figure for Irish Catholics was 43 percent, and for Jews, 59 percent.[14]

Although Greeley and Rossi had observed in 1966 that "it seems very likely that Catholic schools will continue to exist and that Catholics will continue in general to be loyal to them,"[15] vast changes had taken place in the Catholic Church and in its schools between 1964 and 1974 when a second study of parochial school education was conducted by the National Opinion Research Center. In a mere decade, the proportion of children attending Catholic schools at the primary and secondary levels had dropped from 44 to 29 percent—a decline of one-third.[16] Catholic parents still expressed support for Catholic education for their children, yet social mobility had changed many life styles and accelerated the abandonment of urban neighborhoods in favor of suburban areas where public schools were perceived as better than in the cities and where parochial schools simply did not exist. Not only the high costs of building new schools in suburban

[13] Harold Abramson, *Ethnic Diversity in Catholic America* (New York: John Wiley and Sons, 1973), p. 44.

[14] Andrew Greeley, *Ethnicity, Denomination, and Inequality,* Sage Research Papers in the Social Sciences, Series No. 90-029, Vol. 4 (Beverley Hills: Sage Publications, 1976), p. 62.

[15] Greeley and Rossi, *The Education of Catholic Americans,* p. 202.

[16] Greeley, *The American Catholic,* p. 167.

areas, but the added expense of providing increasingly large proportions of lay faculties in existing schools, created a financial crisis for Catholic education. In the mid-1960s, some 100,000 nuns had been teaching for token wages, but in the mid-1970s increasing proportions of lay teachers were required for Catholic schools. By 1977, the Official Catholic Directory showed that there were 50,000 fewer Catholics in the religious life than in 1967, that over 60 percent of the parochial school faculties were made up of lay teachers, that parochial elementary school enrollments were down by 44 percent from 1967, and that diocesan and parochial high school enrollments were down by 22 percent. The only growth area in Catholic education was in attendance at Catholic colleges, which were fewer in number than in 1967 but which enrolled 3 percent more students in those that remained.[17]

The role played by the Irish in the complex saga of American Catholic education cannot be overestimated. Their church leaders had been responsible for the creation of a separate parochial school system and for the establishment of Catholic colleges and universities, and, even though those of other ethnic backgrounds took part as educators and as students, the Irish had been the most fervent supporters. Instead of trying to develop any special pride in the Irish national heritage, the schools had made every effort to Americanize the students and to replace a specific sense of Irishness with a specific sense of what it meant to be a Catholic. In the process, they had been able for many decades to inspire the Irish young to enter the religious life, which has always held high status for the Irish in Ireland and in America; but by the mid-twentieth century the increasing numbers of high school and college-educated American Irish young people were finding secular options more attractive. Attitudes toward those of other ethnic backgrounds had become more liberal, fewer young people entered the religious life, and more moved to the suburbs.

In the final analysis, after a century of Catholic parochial school education, the system seems to have prepared its own demise, as a majority of upwardly mobile Irish Catholics no longer attach great advantage to religious schools. While this "social mobility" thesis goes far in explaining the decline in religious teachers and in attendance at parochial schools for the Irish, it raises new questions about what subsequent impact the decline in Catholic schools will have on more recent Catholic immigrant groups—the Italians, Slovaks, and Poles, for instance—who have not yet reached the status levels of the Irish, and who will find parochial school education less available. To the extent that these ethnic groups are still residents of urban areas where the parochial schools continue to operate, they may find them, as the Irish did, a better preparation for status mobility than the public schools in those areas. But since no other ethnic group has so conscien-

[17] See *The Official Catholic Directory* (New York: P. J. Kenedy and Sons, 1977), General Summary, p. 3.

tiously provided candidates for the religious life, it is questionable whether the parochial schools can continue to operate if the Irish no longer staff them and if they require increased proportions of lay teachers. Thus, the upward mobility of the Irish may have diminished the possibility that other Catholic ethnic groups can use Catholic education in the same way. Time will tell.

## CATHOLIC EDUCATION AND THE INTELLECTUAL SUBSOCIETY

In the 1950s, just as the first sizable cohort of Irish college students was emerging from American colleges and universities, the Russian success in launching "Sputnik" focused attention on what seemed to be a general failure in American education to produce a spirit of scientific inquiry. Schools and colleges nationwide were under attack, but Catholic colleges were particularly criticized for failure to produce students who could make significant scholarly contributions in many areas of intellectual life. In an orgy of self-criticism, Catholic educators admitted that preaching rather than teaching had sometimes prevented the open dialogue that normally is expected among intellectuals and their students. The attitude of self-criticism that prevailed among American educators during the following decade was particularly acute on Catholic campuses. Liberalizing events centered around the "era of the two Johns"—the election of Catholic John Kennedy to the presidency and the ecumenical thrust of Pope John's convening of the Second Vatican Council—which was to have a profound impact on Catholic education as the decade of the 1960s drew to a close. But before discussing those momentous events, let us deal briefly with the nature of the Catholic intellectual subsociety as it existed at that time.

Milton Gordon has hypothesized that even when ethnic subsocieties develop their own parallel social structures to provide for intimate interaction among those of their own group at the various social class levels:

> intellectuals in the United States interact in such patterned ways as to form at least the elementary structure of a subsociety of their own, and . . . this subsociety is the only one in American life in which people of different ethnic backgrounds interact in primary group relations with considerable frequency and with relative comfort and ease.[18]

Since Catholic intellectuals associated with Catholic colleges could be expected to have fewer opportunities to interact easily with those of other ethnic—and especially religious—backgrounds, it would seem likely, then, that this one area of true ethnic merging would be less available to Catholic intellectuals than to others. In research to test this possibility, John D.

[18] Milton M. Gordon, *Assimilation in American Life* (New York: Oxford University Press, 1964), p. 224.

Murray interviewed Catholic academicians in two types of college settings: those in non-Catholic colleges, of whom at least half were Irish, and those in Catholic colleges, of whom about two-thirds were Irish.[19] The Catholic intellectuals on Catholic college campuses were, as might have been expected, oriented more toward a Catholic communal life—drawing more of their close friends from among other Catholic intellectuals, identifying strongly with the Catholic community, maintaining close ties with their extended families, voicing objections to interreligious marriages, and participating regularly at religious services. On the other hand, intellectuals in both college settings recognized the existence of a distinct trans-ethnic subsociety of the kind that Gordon had suggested, and, particularly on the non-Catholic campuses, saw themselves as members of this group. In addition, Catholic intellectuals overall were significantly less traditional in their approach to theology than their nonintellectual counterparts.

Thus, although Catholic intellectuals on Catholic college campuses during the last half of the 1960s seemed less likely to feel themselves part of a broad trans-ethnic intellectual subsociety, yet they were among the least traditional members of the Catholic communal life. This is not surprising when we realize that openness to dialogue with anyone and openness to non-Catholic viewpoints, as well as endorsement of scientific and technical progress, all aspects of membership in a diverse and trans-ethnic subsociety, have been officially condoned by the Catholic Church only since Vatican II. The new emphasis on religious liberty contained in the crucial Declaration of Religious Freedom (largely the work of American Jesuit John Courtney Murray) was only in the mid-1960s beginning to open the way for acceptance of religious liberty as a human right. For intellectuals, the liberty to explore all ideas, including religious ones, was and is basic to academic freedom and is necessary to innovative and productive thought. It may be that the structural separation inherent in separate institutions of higher learning, where many Irish Catholic intellectuals would be found, simply made it more difficult to engage in a learning dialogue. If so, the new openness to discussion and query introduced by Vatican II might well encourage a more conspicuous contribution to American intellectual life on the part of Catholic intellectuals, whether on college campuses or not.

Since higher education represents the only growth area for Catholic education in the late 1970s, it would be helpful to know whether it is the Irish or other ethnic groups who account for the rise in enrollment. It seems plausible to suppose that at least some of the 50,000 Catholics who have opted for a secular rather than a religious life might be attending Catholic colleges instead. If so, the increase in Catholic college attendance by 3 percent might be interpreted as an alternative to the religious life chosen by devout Irish Catholics. This possibility exists, but is not borne out by the

[19] John D. Murray, "The American Catholic Intellectual: An Empirical Test of the Intellectual Subsociety Hypothesis," Unpublished Doctoral Dissertation, University of Massachusetts, 1969.

informal observations of professors in some of these Catholic colleges, especially in the urban East, who report that Catholics from other ethnic groups—notably Italians—are now using higher education as a vehicle for upward mobility in the same way the Irish did a generation ago. If it is true that the Irish were the pacesetters for other Catholic minorities, then it is significant that the kind of Catholic education these later Catholic groups will receive will have been dramatically influenced by those events of the 1960s that changed the course of Catholic thought.

## CHANGES SINCE THE SECOND VATICAN COUNCIL OF 1962–1965

The period from 1960 to 1970 represents probably the most critical ten years in the history of American Catholicism. It began with John F. Kennedy's example in bringing an end to American Catholic sectarianism and withdrawal from the general culture; it moved on to Pope John XXIII's ecumenical spirit, which permeated the Second Vatican Council in Rome; and it came to a close with the 1968 statement on birth control issued by Pope Paul VI—*Humanae vitae*—in which he unexpectedly reaffirmed the traditional Church ban against any form of artificial birth control. It was a decade which saw Catholic priests and nuns marching in civil rights demonstrations, students and parishioners arguing with their priests, members of religious orders leaving the religious life, and nearly all the old truths taught by the Church opened for reinterpretation. The speed with which the average parishioner felt the impact of all these events reflected both the effectiveness of mass communication and the readiness of American Catholics to respond to change.

The changes did not necessarily affect all American Catholics as profoundly as they did the Irish, for each ethnic group within Catholicism has its own orientation based on a unique history. The Irish American orientation had included a defensiveness which originated in efforts to maintain itself in a hostile world, an exaggerated reverence for the clergy who had for centuries been the most trusted and educated leaders in that world, and a compulsion to observe church strictures to the letter—or at least to try. John Cogley sums up the Irish Catholic style as follows:

> The Catholicism of the Irish was generally observant to a fault and comparatively steady and untroubled. It lacked the intellectuality of the French and was neither as cynical about ecclesiastics nor as relaxed about the Faith as the Italian; it was not as absolutistic or mystical as the Spanish, as orderly as the German, or as Nationalistic as the Polish. Unlike other brands of Catholicism, it put central emphasis on strict obedience to ecclesiastical law and on sexual probity.[20]

[20] Cogley, *Catholic America,* p. 147

Through four consecutive autumns, beginning in 1962 and ending in 1965, the Second Vatican Council brought together world Catholic leaders to discuss the future direction of the Church.[21] At the end of the deliberations, American Catholics discovered that they might have more freedom than they had once thought, including religious freedom as a basic human right, a larger role for the laity, a more democratic Church government, and a more accommodative attitude toward the world beyond the Church. They discovered also that Mass would be said in English, that meat might be eaten on Friday, and that many of the strict observances on which the Irish had prided themselves were now to be discarded. The liberating changes introduced by Vatican II coincided with the movement of many Irish Catholics toward a more relaxed accommodation with middle-class American values which had been made possible by John Kennedy's urbane approach to potentially divisive differences between Protestants, Catholics, and Jews.

While some Irish Americans suffered a crisis of faith because the changes had come so fast, others looked forward confidently to the forthcoming decision on the controversial issue of birth control, which the Council, at its conclusion, had passed on for Papal consideration. For many liberal, middle-class young Irish, as well as for many Church leaders, birth control no longer seemed the burning issue it had once been. The decision in favor of family planning had already been made in the privacy of many Catholic homes. But in 1968, *Humanae vitae*—the Papal encyclical which reaffirmed the Church's traditional stand against any form of artificial contraception—shattered the rising expectations of countless American Catholics who had already made a personal decision to live in accordance with the values of non-Catholic middle-class America. For those devout Irish Catholics who had been schooled to be distinctly uneasy about disregarding or disobeying Church strictures, the value conflict between middle-class norms and Church policy was particularly acute.

It is difficult, perhaps impossible, to factor out the many variables that came together to affect Irish Catholics during the momentous decade of the 1960s. At the start of the decade, 66 percent of the Irish were in white collar occupations, 49 percent had attended college, and a youthful Irish Catholic President had moved into the White House. Increased enrollments in parochial schools indicated that Catholics were by no means deserting their belief in the value of religious schools, but in actuality the schools had shown themselves to be more effective in promoting social mobility than in increasing religiosity. At this juncture, the new freedoms emerging from Vatican II promised a future in which policy differences between Catholics and non-Catholics would gradually evaporate. A final mutual acceptance and respect between the Irish and the Anglo Protes-

[21] For a discussion of the Second Vatican Council and its impact on American Catholics, see *ibid.*, Ch. 5.

tants seemed in the offing. If losses in religious orders meant that parochial schools could not be staffed then, reluctantly, American Catholics would do without them. In short, the revolution of rising expectations was too far along when *Humanae vitae* proclaimed that the expectations had gone too far. The 1960s had brought rising expectations for change in many areas of American life—in civil rights, in education, in sexual behavior, in women's rights, as well as in the Catholic Church. In the enthusiasms of the time, expectations had risen faster than they could realistically be satisfied. James Davies has suggested a theory to explain why and when revolutionary reactions occur, as they did in so many areas of American life in the late 1960s and early 1970s.[22] Davies begins by noting that insofar as social change is involved, a gap always exists between the gains expected and the gains actually won; however, as expectations continue to rise—in this case, because of events like Kennedy's election and the new freedoms provided by the Vatican Council—there is hope that the gap between expectations and actual gains will close. If, instead, the gap unexpectedly widens—as it did for many American Catholics following the Papal encyclical against the use of birth control—then it may become critical and result in some form of revolutionary reaction. Catholics did not take to the streets in protest; their revolution was a quiet one. They began to stop attending Church and the monthly confessional; they disregarded *Humanae vitae* in the privacy of their bedrooms; they declared themselves unwilling to accept a position so un-American and so contrary to middle-class values as that pronounced by Pope Paul.

In much the same way that the famine has been described as the final "convincer" for people who were already poised on the edge of decision, so *Humanae vitae* emerged as the final "convincer," in studies conducted at the National Opinion Research Center and interpreted by Andrew Greeley, William McCready, and Kathleen McCourt in *Catholic Schools in a Declining Church.* From data in the 1974 NORC replication of the 1963–64 parochial school study, the researchers found that: (1) the overwhelming majority of American Catholics endorsed the changes of the Second Vatican Council; (2) only about one-sixth of American Catholics supported the Church's teaching on birth control; and (3) the *Humanae vitae* encyclical rather than the Council was responsible for what the authors concluded to be the decline of American Catholicism between 1964 and 1974. Except for the Council, they concluded, the decline would have been even greater [23]

For many years following Max Weber's 1905 proposal in *The Protestant Ethic and the Spirit of Captalism* that religious values are instrumental in determining the nature of economic activity,[24] it had seemed that the

[22] James Davies, "Toward a Theory of Revolution," *American Sociological Review,* 27, No. 1 (February 1962), 5–19.

[23] Andrew Greeley, William McCready, and Kathleen McCourt, *Catholic Schools in a Declining Church* (Kansas City: Sheed and Ward, Inc., 1976), p. 317.

[24] Max Weber, *The Protestant Ethic and the Spirit of Capitalism* (New York: Charles Scribner's Sons, 1958).

values and attitudes inherent in Catholicism simply did not contribute to achievement in a capitalistic society. Comparisons of Protestant and Catholic achievements seemed to verify the belief that Catholics in America were less intellectually courageous and less socioeconomically successful than their Protestant counterparts. The progress of the Irish toward social and economic equality, like that of the later Catholic ethnic minorities, did indeed seem at times imperceptible. But to conclude today that the values contained in the Protestant ethic are as different from Catholic values as they might have appeared in Weber's day is to disregard the movement toward American civil values that has characterized the rising Irish middle class and also to discount the liberalizing forces of Vatican II upon all Catholic ethnic groups in America. That there are still residual differences between the Irish and other Catholics, and between the Irish and the Protestant majority, is not to be denied, but for a group that has progressed through as many stages in the assimilation process as the Irish, there is now relatively little to distinguish the Irish-Catholic ethic from the Anglo Protestant ethic. Religious values may indeed, as Weber demonstrated, affect socioeconomic behavior, but socioeconomic conditions may also, in time, bring about changes in religious values.

C H A P T E R T E N

# Ethnic Identity and Assimilation

America is largely a nation of immigrants and their descendants who, like the Irish, have thrown in their lot with the fortunes of a country far removed from their ancestral home. The assumptions—the hopes—about what would come of this creative mixing of peoples in the process of shaping an American society have varied over the years, but they have nearly always included the belief on the part of all concerned that in time some sort of merging into American society would be possible for most, if not all, ethnic groups.

Even fifty years ago, at a time when immigration had reached such a disturbing peak that defensive quotas had been imposed to curb the influx of southern and eastern Europeans, Robert E. Park nevertheless spoke optimistically about an "apparently progressive and irreversible" cycle characterizing the relations between unlike peoples, which would involve initial contact, then competition, accommodation, and eventually assimilation.[1] Assimilation, then, was to be the goal at the end of the journey—a symbolic passage through a door from ethnic status to total Americanization. Each immigrant group might reach that door at a different time, depending on how long the cultural journey had been; each might be expected to cast off different baggage before passing through; each might receive a different warmth of reception on the other side. But merging would eventually occur.

In the fifty years since Park proposed his "race relations cycle," however, assimilation has come to be recognized as a far more complex process than was once believed. Today we are less likely to ask how long a time full assimilation will require than to ask what form our American pluralism shall take, for it seems far clearer that, in the process of becoming Americans, immigrants and their descendants—individually and as groups—reach and pause at not one but at a series of doors. The assumptions we make and the questions we ask are changed when we are forced to consider kinds and degrees of assimilation, and when we search for the variables that will clarify the nature of each group's experience.

We have already touched upon Milton Gordon's influential conceptual scheme for analyzing the stages of assimilation, and have examined

[1] Robert E. Park, "Our Racial Frontier on the Pacific," in Everett C. Hughes (Ed.), *Race and Culture: Essays in the Sociology of Contemporary Man* (New York: Free Press, 1964), pp. 138–51. Originally published in *Survey Graphic,* 1926.

the key distinction between cultural assimilation and structural assimilation as these applied to the Irish experience.[2] In chapters 4 and 5 we saw that it was the failure to achieve structural assimilation, notably in the areas of old Yankee strength, that promoted the development of parallel Irish Catholic social organizations that both permitted and forced intimate social contacts to remain within the ethnic subsociety. Yet it is apparent that the Irish in America have now reached that stage in the assimilation process where they are free to choose structural assimilation at the level of primary group interaction. Further, the majority appear to have chosen just such a merging into American society.

The Irish provide us with an example of an ethnic group initially considered different enough from the host society to be regarded as "outsiders," but which has now in most respects coalesced with the host society to become "insiders." Because the stages of assimilation are more nearly complete for the Irish than for many other ethnic groups in America, a study of their accommodative maneuvers, as well as the pitfalls they encountered, should clarify both the conditions necessary for transition from one stage to another and the factors influencing the rate of that transition.

To have assumed that assimilation would "just happen" was rather like assuming that a newly married couple would "live happily ever after." Romantic generalizations are as attractive as they are uninformative, but their main disadvantage lies in their tendency to direct attention away from the many crucial variables that might otherwise have been dealt with. In the stages involved in the assimilation process, these variables progress from the most obvious and external differences in cultural style through ever more subtle and internal perceptions about shared values and identity. Because all but the most recent, isolated, or stigmatized minority groups in America have made conspicuous progress in the first stage of cultural or behavioral assimilation, and because many white ethnics stand on the threshold of the second stage of structural or social assimilation, attention has gradually focused on the conditions that either maintain or erode the ethnic subsociety and determine the likelihood of structural assimilation—that stage on which all subsequent forms of assimilation depend. Because there is evidence that Irish Catholics not only are at this threshold, but are moving beyond it, they provide a view of a group in the process of merging into the host society but with their footsteps still fresh enough to trace.

## CULTURAL ASSIMILATION

Two interrelated aspects of Irish Catholic culture presented problems not encountered by earlier Irish settlers of the Ulster migration: Their rural peasant culture was ill-suited for the urban industrial lives they faced in

[2] Milton M. Gordon, *Assimilation in American Life* (New York: Oxford University Press, 1964), Ch. 3, pp. 60–83.

America, and their Catholic faith was at odds with the Protestant ethos of nineteenth-centuryAmerica. The transition from rural peasant to urban industrial worker may well have produced culture shock for many of those uprooted during the famine years, but it was an adaptation with which other Americans were struggling at about the same time, and it did not necessarily involve renunciation of a crucial part of their identity. On the other hand, Catholicism was a cultural characteristic for which the Irish had already paid a heavy price in Ireland and which had, in the process, become highly valued as part of their heritage. Moreover, while culture is, by definition, the entire learned part of inheritance that is transmitted within a social group, religion is one aspect of learned behavior which is ascriptive in nature. The Catholic Church—the strongest supportive institution brought over from Ireland—was linked with Irish history and identity and became the focus of major, enduring cultural differences for the Irish in America.

Possibly the strength of Anglo resistance to Catholicism only served to intensify its importance for the American Irish, who perceived themselves as surrounded by Protestant hostility. Those who might wear their religion lightly under less strained conditions could scarcely avoid responding defensively when Irish Catholicism was attacked, for as Gordon has suggested, "Man defending the honor or welfare of his ethnic group is man defending himself."[3] Quite possibly, the greater the investment already made for that defense, the greater the incorporation of ethnic identity into one's self, and the greater the need to defend the honor of the group. Irish defensiveness was a cultural attribute born of centuries of domination. Nothing in the early experience of the Irish Catholics in America contributed to its rapid erosion.

The acculturation of the famine Irish was seriously retarded because their sheer numbers were bound to disrupt the earlier, settled pattern of social relationships in their adopted communities. The Irish neighborhood groupings which developed out of necessity in shantytowns and city slums and which presented a glaring contrast with the culture of established Anglo-Americans, nevertheless came to provide social satisfactions that were hard to abandon. The reward of such ethnic enclaves found their expression in the nationalistic, religious, and political associations that became the lifeblood of the Irish American community. As the first sizable Catholic immigrant group to pioneer in hostile territory, the Irish may have identified short-cuts for those who followed but they themselves set few records for speed in winning acceptance as fully acculturated Americans.

At the same time, the Irish immigrants were already similar to the

[3] Milton M. Gordon, "Toward a General Theory of Racial and Ethnic Group Relations," in Nathan Glazer and Daniel P. Moynihan (Eds.), *Ethnicity: Theory and Experience* (Cambridge: Harvard University Press, 1975), pp. 84–110.

host society in language and physical features; the majority were young, adaptable, and determined to win acceptance, and they came as permanent settlers rather than as sojourners. The constant communication with the homeland and the continued arrival of new immigrants produced a triple standard for social mobility and success, for while individual Irishmen might feel deprived relative to the Anglo-Americans around them, they might still achieve distinction within their own subsociety, and almost certainly could view themselves as successful relative to their family and friends in Ireland. Time was also in their favor, for the majority arrived while there were substantial economic advantages to be gained by the host society through incorporating the Irish into the economic life of the country. They were the backbone of an industrial expansion the likes of which had never been seen anywhere before. By the time later immigrants arrived in substantial numbers, the Irish had already begun to move into positions of control in labor unions, politics, and church organization. They were in the classic position of being helped up socially by those pushing from below.

To suggest that the American Irish are now culturally assimilated into American life—in their own eyes and in the eyes of the host society—is not to suggest that no culturally distinct traits survive. To become culturally assimilated is not to become identical to the middle-class core culture, which is itself an abstraction to which few Americans of any ethnic background conform completely. To become culturally assimilated is to become similar enough to those in the host society, by social class and by region of the country, so that conflict and discrimination are not provoked by presumed cultural differences.

The conflict and discrimination that formerly attached to religious differences from the Protestant majority have largely subsided for the American Irish. Perhaps this is less because Irish Catholicism has become more "Americanized" and more in line with the Protestant ethic, or even because Protestants have become more understanding of Catholic teachings and less fearful of papal influence, than because religion itself has been transformed from a crucial cultural element to merely one of several acceptable cultural variations in a pluralistic society. What was once socially defined as crucial can later be socially redefined as less important, given the right circumstances. It has taken over a century, but the Irish have lived to see the day when their religious differences pale before their cultural similarities with those of Anglo-American descent.

The gradual development of a Catholic Church which could be viewed by the Protestant host society both as respectable and acceptable has been perhaps one of the greatest Irish contributions to the acculturation of later Catholic immigrants. While the domination of the Catholic Church by the first waves of famine Irish in the mid-1800s raised specters of religious conflicts which might retard what had started as an Americanized form of Catholicism, the extensive organizations associated with the Church also provided an acculturating context for learning how to become American. On balance, there has been little evidence, in spite of Protestant fears to the contrary, that the Irish became less than fully acculturated Americans even though they received their education in parallel Catholic schools, chose Catholic hospitals, or attended Catholic social activities. Indeed, the evidence suggests that the schools effectively stripped the Irish of their peasant heritage in the process of teaching them the skills needed for survival in America, and that while they concentrated on teaching what it meant to be a good Catholic they largely ignored any specific transmission of the Irish heritage.

This need not suggest, however, that the Irish simply abandoned the culture they brought with them and replaced it with a pre-formed American culture, for cultural elements flow both ways, and through the process of syncretism are combined into new shapes. Working within the American political framework, the Irish united American processes and Irish styles to develop the highly structured urban political machines which dominated the period of urban growth. Working within the American framework of compulsory education, they created an alternative, Church-sponsored educational system. Working within the social and physical boundaries of urban development, they created alternative social structures to serve their ethnic communities in countless American cities. For later immigrants, these new shapes of political, educational, and social life were already part of an existing American cultural pattern. These later groups not only adapted to them, but made their own subtle changes, all of which were incorporated into American culture just as the Irish song, the Irish humor, the Irish bar, and the wearing of the green on Saint Patrick's Day had been.

To suggest that there are persistent ethnic traits that distinguish the Irish today as culturally different in any distinctive way may be to focus on those residual ethnic enclaves that remain as holdovers from an earlier time—especially among those who have been by-passed in the general movement of the group toward more complete acculturation. Such Irish enclaves do exist, with all the defensiveness needed to make them conspicuous targets for those who wish to attach ancient free-floating stereotypes to some contemporary referent. Characteristic ethnic traits may also be identified in attitude and value orientations that persist as part of a style of child rearing, religious belief, political viewpoint, or more generalized world view that is more often displayed by those who identify themselves as Irish than among those who do not. Such statistical variations do exist, though earlier chapters have shown that the American Irish have not only moved toward conformity with American cultural traits in most respects but have in some respects overconformed. But except for those who have remained in ethnically enclosed sections of American cities, or who have just arrived from Ireland, the cultural assimilation of Irish Americans appears to be virtually complete.

### STRUCTURAL ASSIMILATION

Because structural assimilation is by definition integration on a large scale with the host society at the primary group level—in other words, acceptance into cliques, clubs, and institutions such that comfortable friendships may develop and necessary business contacts may be made—it may be thought of as the crucial threshold to later stages of assimilation. Immigrants who have considered themselves fully acculturated and totally Americanized have been made to wait at this particular door without being admitted, for a major distinction between cultural and structural assimilation is that the former is under the control of the ethnic group itself whereas the latter is ultimately under the control of the host society.

Individuals may proceed on their own to adapt to the culture of the host society, and may be accepted on their own special merits as atypical members of their ethnic group, but if structural assimilation becomes widespread the host society has, in effect, opened the door to all subsequent forms of assimilation, of which intermarriage is the most obvious and the most imminent. Hence the caution on the part of those already "there" about admitting the newcomers to the inner circles. On the secondary level of jobs, intermixing can and often does occur, as cultural assimilation permits; however, unless structural assimilation follows, the ethnic group member will find his most intimate relationships still limited to the ethnically separate social world of family, friends, and neighborhood. Thus, the bars at the door of structural assimilation are formidable ones, because the doors must be opened from the far side.

The Irish Catholics were acculturated to American life, though religiously distinct, long before they were free to share the social world of the host society on any extensive basis. During these years of exclusion, the development of parallel social structures reflected the need for interpersonal contact at all social class levels, and even led, in time, to an elite Irish "society" which mirrored that of the Anglo-American upper class. Because structural assimilation is now recognized as the crucial variable, it has been discussed extensively in previous chapters, along with variations in degree of structural merging as a consequence of region, generation in this country, social class level, and religious affiliation. Those Irish who live outside New England, who have been several generations in America, who are economically secure, and whose Catholicism does not completely define their social boundaries find few if any barriers raised to prevent social merging.

The dramatic decline in availability of Catholic schools in areas where Irish Catholics now live suggests that friendship formation and comfortable social contacts in other areas of life will proceed at an even more rapid rate in the years to come. The additional erosion of distinguishing rituals and beliefs that once set Catholics and Protestants so far apart, and the gradual loss of vitality in old institutionalized religious forms (though not necessarily in newer communal forms which draw converts from different religious backgrounds) seems likely also to speed up the process. The recognition of a new and more liberal political style that emerged during Kennedy's presidency further weakens the perception of Irish politicians as at odds with the Anglo-American political style. The gradual incorporation of Irish upper-class families, Irish intellectuals, and Irish business and professional leaders into existing host society institutions indicates that the structural boundaries are permeable and that large-scale entrance into cliques, clubs, and institutions of the host society is possible, but of course not mandatory.

Because ultimately structural assimilation rests on choice—first by the host society in opening the doors and then by the ethnic group in choosing whether or not to pass through—a resurgence of interest in the social position of white ethnics like the Irish has centered around whether or not ethnic identity and ethnic subsociety are too valuable to be abandoned. Some suggest that people have, after all, too much basic good sense to throw away their ethnic anchorages in return for a homogenized American identity; others suggest that American life is too complex to provide a simple "American" identity at all. Good sense or not, the Irish may already have moved beyond the point of no return, and may have concluded that their ethnic anchorage is simply American rather than Irish, or even Irish American. Lawrence McCaffrey expresses a lingering doubt about the wisdom of all this when he asks: "Is the history of Irish-America an ethnic success story or a warning to other groups that they should be wary of surrendering ethnicity for the sake of assimilation?"[4] For many Irish Americans enthusiastically taking part in the "success story" this is an academic question best left to scholars. Their choices have already been made.

While it is surely time to be aware that past and present exclusionary policies on the part of a dominant society can prevent a structural assimilation that is earnestly desired by minority groups and can force the development of ethnic communities with parallel ethnic institutions and social bonds, it is possible to exaggerate the necessity for these ethnic bonds among groups who feel themselves to be completely Americanized. Richard Alba, in his study of assimilation among various Catholic ethnic groups, has pointed to the hazards of assuming that ethnic communality is widespread simply because we know that some ethnically homogeneous communities exist and because we have studied them, since "the mere persistence of ethnic neighborhoods does not indicate that most members of a given ancestry group live in such neighborhoods, nor does it disprove that

[4] Lawrence J. McCaffrey, *The Irish Diaspora in America* (Bloomington: Indiana University Press, 1976), p. 10

social assimilation is widespread among those outside of ethnic neighborhoods.[5] The persistence of Irish neighborhoods in American cities is as well known as is their gradual abandonment by those who have the option of leaving them. In other words, to say that the ethnic subsociety can persist as a viable alternative even after structural assimilation has become widespread is not to say that it is preferable. Support groups in one form or another appear to be a psychological necessity, but communal bonds can and do form along lines of achievement as well as along lines of ascription. The intellectual subsociety which transcends ethnic origins is as much an anchorage as the ethnic subsociety which provides another kind of anchorage. One is not necessarily preferable to the other.

## BEYOND STRUCTURAL ASSIMILATION

The barriers to full assimilation have largely fallen for the Irish in America. Intermarriage is higher than for any other ethnic group, with a consequent mixture of ethnic backgrounds which has diluted the meaning of Irish American identity. Thus, large-scale marital assimilation has not only emerged from structural assimilation but has also contributed to it, as kinship networks have come to include Americans with different ethnic identities. Identificational assimilation—the development of a sense of peoplehood based exclusively on the host society—is difficult to measure, since those who are asked to indentify their land of origin may choose from a mixed ancestry to identify themselves with one of several ancestral origins but may also choose to call themselves simply Old American. Just as the majority of Protestant Scotch-Irish have assumed an American identity, so also may the descendants of later Catholic Irish do the same. With the end of nationalist concern for Irish freedom on the part of most American Irish, full identification with American life became possible and was enthusiastically pursued by most Irish in America. Prejudice and discrimination are virtually unknown by Irish Americans now overwhelmingly in their third or later generation in this country. Even at the national level, Kennedy's presidency demonstrated for once and all that Irish Catholics were, above all, Americans, and since that time value conflicts of Church versus state have lost their power to inflame passions. In the two most obvious areas of civic controversy—the issues of parochial school support and birth control or abortion policies—the majority of Irish Catholics cannot be roused to take an effective stand, for these are no longer perceived as the burning issues they once appeared to be.

It seems likely that in the years to come, the Irish American

[5] Richard D. Alba, "Social Assimilation Among American Catholic National-Origin Groups," *American Sociological Review,* 41 (December 1976), 1032.

experience will serve as a model for other ethnic groups of how gradual assimilation can occur. Whether this 150-year saga—with its share of conflict and discrimination as well as its share of cooperation and success—will serve to chart a useful path for other ethnic groups with different kinds of problems remains to be seen. What the Irish have demonstrated is that American life can encompass difference without insisting on eradicating it, and that an ethnic group can adopt an American identity without completely renouncing its historical sense of peoplehood. Other groups may test the limits of American willingness to tolerate such differences, and may confront their own willingness to adopt an American identity with other results, but the experience of the Catholic Irish in America has charted a path that has, at the very least, suggested what the options might be.

# *Index*

A



B



C

R



S



T



U



V

### W



### Y



### Z